Alan Swallow and his daughter, Karen. Portland, Oregon, 1966.
Photograph by William Stafford.

Publishing in the West:
ALAN SWALLOW

Some Letters and Commentaries

~~~~~~

Edited, with an Introduction by,

WILLIAM F. CLAIRE

~~~~~~

The Lightning Tree, Inc., Jene Lyon, Publisher

Post Office Box 1837
Santa Fe, New Mexico 87501

ACKNOWLEDGEMENTS

The editor gratefully acknowledges permission from the estate of the late Alan Swallow, Denver, Colorado, for use of the poem and letters quoted. The poem, "For Mae," appeared in *The Remembered Land,* The Press of James A. Decker, Prairie City, Illinois, Copyright 1946 by Alan Swallow. Much appreciation is due to the recipients of the letters quoted, who made available the original documents, to Marcella M. du Pont for the quotation used in the Editor's Introduction and to The Princeton University Library and Allen Tate for the Tate letters.

Library of Congress Catalog Card Number:
73-89794

ISBN: 0-89016-003-1

*Printed in the United States of America
at The Lightning Tree*

THE LIGHTNING TREE, INC.   JENE LYON, PUBLISHER
P. O. Box 1837, Santa Fe, New Mexico 87501   U. S. A.

FOR MAE

How shall I sing our love? In vain
Would we bring utterance of song to bed,
For love will never know the pulse of rain
Or answer time considered, counted, fled.

Our love would better find epitome
In living, season placed on season, spring
On fall and fall on spring, deliberately.
We both to still event of seed should bring
Not striving after birds or waft of feather
But quiet of our living two together.

It will not matter that the earth, or sky,
Or any sea are never ours alone.
It is enough that we can turn an eye
Upon the world and see the sun on stone.
It is enough that we can see the night
Come down, and will not feel the need of light.

Alan Swallow

CONTENTS

CONTENTS

INTRODUCTION William F. Claire

William F. Claire is the founding editor and publisher of *Voyages: A National Literary Magazine.* He has written extensively on contemporary literature. His essays and poetry have appeared in many journals and anthologies. He is the author of *The Strange Coherence of Our Dreams,* Poems by William F. Claire, with woodcuts by Adele Aldridge, and "That Unpredictable Bloom: The Poetry of Katherine Garrison Chapin." Mr. Claire was born in Northampton, Massachusetts, educated at Columbia University, and is currently Director of the Washington office of the State University of New York.

The name Alan Swallow, to poets, publishers and lovers of the printed word, symbolizes the best tradition of an American literary culture. It is a name that suggests to many people a man who remained apart from the commercial claques of his day and sensitive to the needs of writers in a way that will probably not be matched by another publisher with his long-range objectives. For Swallow was determined to print, publish and distribute books widely on an independent basis—a virtually one-man attempt to make an impact on his times in the precarious and often perverse world of publishing. The list of writers he published attests to his accomplishments, and his sudden death at the age of 51 was a shattering blow to quality publishing. His name goes on now in a publishing house in Chicago—a good one—but some worlds die with some men, and Alan Swallow's rests peacefully with his ashes near the western mountains of Colorado he loved so well.

"We come to earth for romance," a Swallow author has written, and "a great romance sustains us." Alan Swallow was in love with books, with type and with the written word. Nothing could prevent the bringing together of the component parts of this romance into a life-long love affair, which became, under various imprints, Alan Swallow, Publisher. When he died at his typewriter —on Thanksgiving Day in 1966—he was mourned by people across the nation who knew him as an American original, as rare as those vanishing species of western wildlife.

His uniqueness is evident in his letters, with their wisdom, their sincerity and their unfailing enthusiasm. He was quite simply a very special editor for any number of talented writers who might never have received even a preliminary reading—many because of the experimental nature of their writing—from the large commercial houses. No human being spent more time with more writers to better purpose than Alan Swallow. This is evidenced in the letters selected here. His qualities as a human being are attested to in the tributes written for this collection by Anaïs Nin (a writer whom Swallow published when others would not consider her), and James Schevill (whom Swallow encouraged and published).

Nin, whose now famous Diary was first jointly published by Alan Swallow and Harcourt, Brace & World, is one among many writers whom Swallow kept in print or first published. Others include Schevill, J. V. Cunningham, Vardis Fisher, Allen Tate, Thomas McGrath, Frank Waters and Yvor Winters, to name just a few.

Alan Swallow wrote literally thousands of long letters in his short life; an indication of his enormous energy and concern for both his authors and friends. The few letters selected here—covering a range of topics and sent to very different people over nearly 25 years—offer, I believe, important glimpses into his life, and all relate to the history and development of Alan Swallow, Publisher. Because they do, they represent a running historical commentary on a unique aspect of American publishing in the West and its impact on the entire country.

The letters are arranged by recipient and chronologically by the first date in each series. They start at the time Swallow was faced with military induction in the early 1940's and end with the "Dear Author" letters of the 1960's. They trace the development of the original Swallow press and cover most of the significant aspects of his life. The numerous physical problems that wore him down in the end became a recurring theme in his letters—the wonder being that he never gave up. And as Mark Harris noted in a *New York Times* memorial piece on Swallow, he never sold out.

The letters to Ann Stanford are included in a tight selection to demonstrate how Swallow worked with one author over a period of time, an important period for Stanford who was then unknown. They concern themselves with her first two books, her attitude as a disciple of Yvor Winters and other facets of a publisher communicating with a young poet.

The letters to Allen Tate trace the beginning of a long friendship that started when Swallow was two years out of graduate school and interested in publishing an anthology selected from literary magazines. Later on Swallow was to become important in Tate's publishing career, and Tate himself acknowledged that he owed his life in print as a critic to Alan Swallow. The letters build to a triumphant note in a postcard (always a Swallow favorite means of communication) that, having obtained the rights to publish a Tate paperback book of poems, "I feel Swallow Paperbooks will then have the three best poets alive in America!" (I presume he meant Winters, Cunningham and Tate.)

The long letter to A. H. Reiter in New York is in response to a series of suggestions to Swallow on how he should have been promoting his books, particularly a series by Vardis Fisher. The reply is vintage Swallow. . .factual, straightforward, sometimes testy, always sincere. Letters to Natalie Robins and Martin Robbins return to the themes of the letters to Stanford and Reiter: his desire to help the individual writer, and his constant worries over the distribution of his books.

The two letters and postcard to Roger Hecht cover interesting aspects of Swallow—his lack of belief in the standard introduction or jacket blurb on a book, and his admonition to Hecht not to "worry about readings." And another note, in September 1966, expresses some fear of an expanding publishing schedule that Swallow is attempting to make "manageable once more." Hecht has appended a short note which amounts to a tribute to the man who began his publishing career.

A single letter to the poet Richard Gillman is more vintage Swallow: the type of letter meant to shore up a writer's strength, in this case not to worry about reviews of his book, or the absence of them.

The first general letter sent by Swallow to his authors in 1962 is historically important in many ways, in that it traces the early development of the Swallow press and publishing in the West. The end of the relationship between Swallow and the Johnson Publishing Company of Boulder, Colorado, was to begin a new aspect of Swallow's life explained in his later letters, a kind of oral commentary on the fortunes of his press, which evolved in such a way that by late 1963 he was literally begging for assistance—his first appeal of any kind—for "any equipment to be able to help in production of a book of poems in 1964." This desire to honor commitments, to keep publishing, came after a coronary attack and the recurrence of old injuries from a motorcycle accident. The letter of October 1965 continues the litany of problems of the press, written by a man who had suffered much but who still could say, ". . .as a person of large energy, I can do much."

The final letter included here dated February 1, 1966, is, I believe, the last letter of its kind written by Swallow before his death. It gives a historical chronology of his publishing career, filling in the gaps of some of the earlier letters, and demonstrating without question that he was a man of large ambition, and a man of considerable energy and attainment. . .culminating in the announcement of the joint publishing imprint of The Swallow Press and Harcourt, Brace & World for the first volume of *The Diary of Anäis Nin: 1931-1934.* While this temporary marriage to the big New York publishing world must have been gratifying, it is clear from this final letter that what mattered to Swallow were the events listed in the chronology of his fascinating publishing career.

The poet Roger Hecht has made the poignant observation that Swallow had the rare quality of writing to each individual as though that person were the only one who mattered. Time after time Swallow gave his thoughts and criticism to aspiring writers, many of whom were communicating with a publisher for the first time. His responses were never perfunctory.

These letters then serve as a further indication of the kind of man Alan Swallow was—they can be read now with a mixture of wonder and regret. They constitute—in this form—perhaps the only effort since his tragic death (apart from the memorial tributes and a special issue of *The Denver Quarterly*—Spring, 1967, Vol. II, No. 1) to place in some historical context the importance of the Swallow experiment in the development of our contemporary literary culture.

The editor owes deep gratitude to Mrs. Swallow, who gave permission at the outset, and to whom this collection is indirectly dedicated, not only by the introductory poem, but also by its subject, who will be remembered as long as people care about the unique ingredients of independence, taste and faith that came to symbolize the name and personality of Alan Swallow.

WASHINGTON, D. C.

ALAN SWALLOW   Anaïs Nin

Anaïs Nin was born in Paris, the daughter of Spanish composer-pianist Joaquin Nin and Rosa Culmell Nin. Her first book, *D. H. Lawrence: An Unprofessional Study*, was published in Paris in 1932, and later issued in the U. S. by Alan Swallow. Among her many books are *House of Incest, Winter of Artifice, Under a Glass Bell, Ladders to Fire, A Spy in the House of Love, The Novel of the Future* and her renowned *Diary*, now in its fifth volume. She was an original advisory editor of *Voyages. Under the Sign of Pisces*, published at Ohio State University, chronicles the activities of her life and the circle of her friends.

Every story of devotion and integrity begins with a story of love and gratitude. Alan Swallow was born on an irrigated farm in northwestern Wyoming. He was an omnivorous reader. As in many lives not too rich in incidents, books became a form of travel, knowledge, expansion, adventure and enrichment. So at the base of the admirable harmony of his life lies the love of books, a recognition of their value. He worked at a filling station and in between customers he read Haldeman-Julius Publications because they were available to his budget.

"I was tremendously attracted by several things that I learned then: first by the effort of Haldeman-Julius to provide good literature at inexpensive prices—and I suppose that there was planted a small seed of the idea of publishing at some time; second through Haldeman-Julius' publications of magazines and through reading other materials, I became aware of the group we call 'The Little Magazines.' I was certainly impressed with the idealism and the effort of these magazines to put out a quality work without consideration for commercial results."

Many young men have started such idealistic schemes, and many printing presses were inaugurated, but very few were carried into maturity and full expansion as Alan Swallow, Publisher. He had more courage, more persistence and more dedication.

In 1939 he borrowed a hundred dollars from his father and

secured a second-hand five-by-eight Kelsey handpress. This was set up in the garage of the apartment where he lived.

This was the beginning.

This was the outline of his activity. What I could read of his character from our long correspondence and only one meeting was the enthusiasms which sustained and recharged him, his delight in his victories, his obstinacy in struggling against the established ways of publication which would seem unconquerable by an individual. The solidity and intelligence in his activity were derived not only from his individual conviction, integrity and obstinacy; it came from his love of writing and his wisdom about writing. He knew that it was his attitude and his construction in publishing which alone would keep quality writing alive. He knew that commercial publishing was the worst enemy of the writer and that this could not be obscured by the example of a few writers materially enriched who so often were quickly emasculated and sterilized by the system, and ceased to be writers altogether.

Perhaps because he was a man from the West, born close to the earth, because he was brought up on the solidity of certain eternal values, he knew the simple truths which commerce so often overlooks. Commerce never concerns itself with seedling, crops, growth, but only with the finished object to be sold. It never concerns itself with the possible dangers of writers dying out, writing dying out. Commerce does not bother with research, experiment, the need for renewal, the protection for writing which may not yield immediate gain. A writer takes too long to grow! Alan Swallow was an educator, among other things, and this may have given him his sense of the future. This is a very important feature in the history of his achievements. He knew that writers needed to be free of exorbitant economic pressure and demand put upon them by commercial publishers, the gruesome test of quick sales, immediate acceptance, of the figures added like figures on a Wall Street ticker tape.

An image comes to my mind when I seek a parallel to his activities. The woodcutting companies buy land, cut down all the trees, and pass on to buy another sector of the forest, leaving the one they decimated like an ugly empty cemetery. The Forest Service, led by another idealist, Gifford Pinchot, came along to re-plant the devastated land (a devastation which caused floods and droughts) and to teach selective cutting of the mature trees and not the young ones, so as to give the young ones time to grow. The forests were saved from ugly gashes, destroyed land, and so was the future of the trees themselves.

Alan Swallow applied this earthy principle to his publishing. Possibly because he was himself a poet, he also knew that poetry was the fecundating seed of all writing. He was an idealist but not a romantic. The source of his contentment, his philosophical equilibrium and energy, was his wisdom, his pride in growth. He enjoyed the challenge of the difficulties. At one time individual effort was highly regarded in America. Then for a time it was denigrated. Now it has been recognized once more by the direct success of underground films, underground presses, underground theatre; and the Giant Industries were revealed as empty factories while the underground fed its depleted coffers. So once more, individual effort is restored to its proper place; it is the research department of all achievements, for future enrichment of all.

I never saw Alan Swallow waste a moment of anger at commercial publishers. He simply thought they were mistaken in their own self-interest. Shortsighted. He was more intent on creating his own structure which would embody his earthy wisdom. He was a man capable of devotion, selflessness, integrity, but he was practical. His solutions were effective. He proved a man could support his family and yet create a publishing house of impressive achievements. The commercial publishers were ultimately destroying the very source of their wealth. Writers succumbed first of all to a false dream of wealth which only a few would attain, then to a hothouse forcing of their talents, then to a star system which continued to publish the most mediocre work of any writer who had attained a reputation. This meant that the system was destructive to the life of writing itself. Good writers were caught in an absurd race for quick sales, false publicity, and if they failed to pass the first harsh test of economic exigencies they were considered failures. Some of these writers came to Alan Swallow. He made minimal demands on them. He was patient with them. They continued to expand and develop and several among them were recognized as valuable by Big Business later.

His *An Editor's Essays of Two Decades* reveals a quiet sense of basic values, a classical critical faculty, and a devotion to this very regional, native, folkloric literature which has always been at the roots of all national literature. This essentially American literature which the merchandising East wanted so much to produce was actually fed and sustained not by them but by such underground, independent methods. Small magazines, small publishers, private ventures, young presses, kept writing alive even though some of them did not survive.

The only discouragement I ever saw in Alan Swallow was due to his physical handicaps: his heart attack and his leg injury. He could not reduce his activity because it was an expression of his entire personality.

Some people feel that the great burden of an individual achievement killed him. I am not certain about this. When a man has such a need of working at something he believes in, in harmony with his ideas, temperament and convictions, any other form of life would have killed him sooner. True, he might have been helped more. One wishes he had lived longer, to enjoy his victories. But he was given time to make a unique synthesis of all his many talents, as a poet, essayist, critic, teacher and editor, and as a man of action who needed a concrete proof of his service to writing.

Letters to Authors and Others

LETTERS TO ANN STANFORD

Ann Stanford is an American poet and translator whose most recent collection of poetry, *The Descent,* was published by The Viking Press, Inc. In 1972 she received an Award in Literature from The National Institute of Arts and Letters-The American Academy of Arts and Letters. She teaches at San Fernando Valley State College.

GUNNISON, COLORADO
December 15, 1942

Dear Miss Stanford,

Forgive me for not writing you sooner after receiving your ms. The reason is that my situation is very uncertain at the moment. Soon after I wrote you suggesting that you send the ms., I received notice to take my preliminary physical examination. At the moment, it seemed a possibility that I might be called this month. Several circumstances, however, combined to throw off the time schedule. My examination here was late, so that the results were available to my draft board in Albuquerque only last week. In addition, the college has requested my deferment for the school year. I had thought that the draft board would review my case and I would be reclassified. . .; but so far no reclassification has come. What it will be, I do not know, though it is difficult to make out a case for an English teacher being in a critical occupation, and I expect it to be 1-A, subject to immediate call— which would probably mean call next month. That is as much as I know, and much of it, as you see, is guesswork.

I don't need to say that I would like very much to publish your collection of poems. I admire them very much. But what I can do is not certain, and I have been able, because of this uncertainty of status, only to hazard certain possibilities according to various dispositions of my case. (My draft status is further complicated by the fact that Mrs. Swallow is expecting a child the last of this month. As you see, it is difficult to have a definite notion of what will happen until I hear definitely from the board.) If I am called, I have in mind immediately getting in touch with Decker [The Press of James A. Decker, then of Prairie City, Illinois] to see if he won't take on the book. That might be the easiest thing to do anyway, if he would take it. I have also thought of approaching him with a suggestion for a joint publication, in which each of us would stand half the expense. But the only way that would work out is that I would have to put up my half in the form of cash, and he would put up his half in the form of work. And, if anything, it needs to be the other way round.

Of course what happens is completely contingent upon my draft status. But if I can stay here during the school year, I am confident I could handle the printing end. The question would be the binding. I think the edition ought properly to be limited to about 200 copies—you are not widely known, and that is what counts in sales, not quality of verse. Now I could get a good cloth binding for about 35 cents per copy, probably somewhere between $60 and $70 for the 200 copies. I have thought that a good paper cover—done not as a pamphlet, but with a square back, with sections sewed, etc., as in a full book—might be a good way of handling the volume, keeping the cost low, being attractive. That could be done for less than half the cost of full cloth binding. I have in mind the style used often for books of poems in England and on the Continent—a friend sent me such a book just recently, very attractive and to the point for poetry. But it still isn't a cloth binding.

When I suggested 48 pages, I had in mind the total number of pages for the book, including introductory pages, etc. Your ms. would require about 74 pages altogether, with your numbered sections, introductory pages, etc. But no matter—it is a good ms., and if it is to be a book, it might as well be the whole thing; the alternative would be a pamphlet pure and simple, and would necessitate cutting. J. V. Cunningham's introductory poem is nice; probably he is right about an introduction, this poem serving the purpose as well or better.

I'm sorry that I can't be more definite about the matter now. If you would like to try the ms. somewhere else, I'll return it. I should know something rather definite before too long, however, and I'm very interested in it and will do all I can to see that it is published.

Cordially,

Alan Swallow

DENVER, COLORADO
March 25, 1954

Dear Ann,

We had a brief vacation to Albuquerque, first of its kind in a long while; and I returned to find your letter of March 16. It must have arrived here the day we left. It was certainly welcome, as always from you.

In the accumulated mail were three more orders for *The White Bird* [a book of poems by Stanford]; the first three this year. The card device is certainly effective, and I think you are quite right in using them as you do. No one is forcing the sale; I suppose some would be just as happy if they never heard of it; but a volume of poems is occasionally appreciated and can only be known by such small devices. I think I must have explained my idea of a poet's reputation moving by concentric circles!

. . . .

I don't blame you for wanting to do something else. This is probably the proper procedure. I think you'll have to admit that the [Yvor] Winters type of advice and help makes of a young poet a conscientious practitioner; it also makes him write with a great deal more purity of language, or whatever you would want to call it. (I know a good bit about this, for I had almost exactly the opposite kind of training when I started to write poetry, insofar as I had any training at all.) But the problems for the poet after he has mastered the beginning (and written several extremely remarkable poems, as you have) are just as serious, and the poet has to work on his own idiom as it must differentiate itself from the learned, perhaps somewhat imitative behavior. But I do not think you should think of this as "escape." This is off the cuff, but I suppose I think of the matter in two ways: First, there is in each of us a spark of that devilish but delightful desire to kick over the reins of any authority, however gentle (and sometimes the gentle authority most delightfully kicked over); I think you have a bit of this spark in you, and I honor you for it. It is one of the principles by which I live, I think. Second, and probably most important, we seek the good (in this case, accomplishment as poet, to the best of our abilities), and when the training is good, or the influence of someone is good (mine was mostly bad, I suspect, and yours mostly good), we do not want too much to overthrow the good as learn to make it individually our own, adapted, in the end, in our own manner. But it is not escape. This reminds me of your nice comment on two ways to write a poem—something of this sort I have told my students about the poem and the story . . .over-simplified, to make a neat antithesis—to proceed from idea to embodiment; to proceed from "experience" to the idea of the experience. In these two or three paragraphs of yours, I think you put the matter excellently well. But my parallel for the moment is with one's self. To stretch the metaphor—one must make a poem of one's self the second way as well as the first. I think you are trying that way now.

But you are too good a poet for me to be lecturing. I don't like to lecture, anyway—just picking up from comments of your own. And I'm giving over the teaching for a time, as you heard . . .effective August 31, the resignation. I'll stick on in Denver for a time, at least. The publishing has been growing on me—a little in the literary titles, after long persistence and finally ending up, unwanted by me, as almost the sole independent outlet for poetry and criticism; but chiefly with the regional titles—so that I can't manage it part-time as before. For the first time I can think of taking some money from it, but I can't afford to hire labor. So I'll let it have its head a bit (within the limited capital that I can possibly find to work with) while I am also getting some of my own postponed work done. Then after a couple years, as I plan now, I'll make the best arrangements for the publishing —quit it, pull it down arbitrarily to a few things, or hire some labor to help carry it on—and then get back to teaching, somewhere. But we'll see.

Cordially,

Alan

DENVER, COLORADO
May 1, 1956

Dear Ann,

Please forgive me for such a late reply to your letter of April 27—mailed May 1. I truly enjoyed it and the feeling of getting in touch with your thinking and feeling. And I have reread it and thought about it a good bit as I worked away at the pretty darned big publishing program I have for this year. (By the way—I'm sorry the information didn't get to you—I resigned from the University of Denver effective August, 1954, to work full-time, for a while, at publishing. I say "for a while" because I've always felt that I cannot publish the things I want to publish and make a living, however poor a one, considering family obligations. However, after some 13 years or so of making a living elsewhere and putting a lot of time and as much money as I could afford into the publishing, finally in 1954 it was earning a bit, and I took some out; it had grown so that I just couldn't feel I could do my formerly good job (I hoped!) of teaching and keep up the publishing, too. So I decided to give the publishing a stronger try, let it have a full chance for a time, to see what would happen. The case is very much up in the air after nearly two years. But— except that those jobs open only one time a year!—I can always go back to teaching, which I love very much; but when and if I do, I'll have to cut the publishing back to a smaller thing that I can possibly manage in part-time; now I can't manage it full time!)

I liked what you said about *Magellan* [a book by Ann Stanford: *Magellan: A Poem To Be Read By Several Voices,* 1958]. I think you have a pretty good perspective on it now—both regarding its "failures" and what aspects of the original conception you must hold to and improve to get rid of the failures. I think I agree pretty much along the line with what you have said—that a revision might stand. The only real problem troubling me, yet, is the thematic one. I can't quite see Magellan standing for a symbol of the human will—or even, I guess (and this is the real problem for me), that this in itself is a worthy theme. Supposing, for a moment, that this were decided as adequate, I did feel that you overloaded the work with more than this, much more nebulous, but sort of reaching out to the stars kind of thing that would elevate Magellan even higher in the firmament. It was difficult to put one's finger on, and I never felt that I did. So the thematic thing, as I see it, is double-edged: (a) is the theme about the human will adequate enough for a "large" poem? And (b) have you really dealt with that theme or clouded it by other things? These are just matters you may want to think about more as you pick up the poem again after a time of writing shorter poems.

About the general direction in your work. . .I can understand your impatience about being classified as Yvor Winters' disciple. As you say, no one is rational about Winters—one of his great feats has been to disturb people, to shake them so that they become angry. Sometimes then they come to see better; sometimes they never learn more—as Jarrell in speaking of Fitzell [Lincoln Fitzell, one of the first poets published by Swallow in 1940], who was never ever a Winters disciple and wrote his best and most characteristic poems before he had any more than heard of Winters. (I wrote to the *Saturday Review* about this, the first time and only time I broke my pledge not to write to reviewers of books I published, because the reviewer there had said Fitzell was a member of that group and then attacked the group! At least the facts ought to be straight.) In a way, though, I think you took the reviewers of your book too seriously. For example, Rolfe Humphries—whom I really like and admire; I considered him the only decent reviewer of poetry on a regular basis, and then the *Nation* had to give him up! I just don't think that the idea he suggested—flouting instruction in some aspect of the poem while holding it in another—is workable at all. For any kind of instruction. Surely this idea that the opposition of the younger generation to an older ought to be automatic—and by being automati will result in better verse!—is a bit absurd—that is, insofar as a few reasonably known things are concerned. Sure, I'm great for revolt—but in poetry to assume that there is some progress by revolting against a method or insight is silly. The method may be the way to write a fine poem; the revolt would be to a method resulting in a poorer poem. The logic of the position these people take just won't hold water. Now then, I fully realize that there is a point, indeed, at which one must step out on his own. As you know, I never studied with Winters, and I never learned to write poems the way he apparently wants. But I can see clearly that some of the attitudes I did receive from people such as Robert Penn Warren were not sound at all—I knew it at the time, but not so well as I knew it considerably later when I found some of the attitudes hard to shrug off.

I go round and round and haven't said this very well. It is a ticklish problem. But what it boils down to is that I am pretty confident that the way is not one of direct revolt—and certainly not to method in the deepest sense—but to find one's own attitudes about the world, which become the subject matter of the poems and emotions of the poems. That is a bigger problem, probably, than the literary one of attitudes toward poetry, method, etc. Like you, I've got sick and tired of the literary quarterlies; I practically never read them anymore, for they are now so repetitive and so narrow—but a Winters would agree with this entirely, I'm sure. The stultification in them comes from weak absorption of a lot of poor ideas, and a pure second-generation mockery of vigor without being able to see in what ways even the "pioneer" vigor was misdirected at times. One reason for my starting *Twentieth Century Literature* [a magazine published by Swallow] was to have something which would return to basic things about discussing the literature, rather than the pattern established by the literary quarterlies. There was a real honey of these in the last *Sewanee*, which I received because of the review—in which the reviewer, a young guy who got one of their fellowships, etc., took on a large list of new volumes of poems, had McGrath's [Thomas McGrath, poet] first (as worst) and ended up with a claim that Jarrell is now a great poet. I know the reasoning and "taste" which is exhibited in this work, for my graduate study lay in that general background of attitude. But the guy has made himself blind as a bat—as we say, he doesn't know his ass from a hole in the ground. He can't see the kind of vitality which does lie in McGrath's work, whatever its faults (which are often many); likewise, the training makes him lack the irony or perspective to see how mannered and weak Jarrell is in his verse.

Anyway, I shall most certainly be interested in seeing the batch of poems, and I'll try to be a lot more specific than this jotting of some random thoughts in response to your comments. A few particulars right now: Donald Hall was at Stanford for a while and studied for a while with Winters; he shows this only some of the time in his verse, it seems—I know of some in magazines; Edgar Bowers, whose collection is now at the bindery, was runner-up in the Lamont thing [The Lamont Poetry Prize for a first volume of poems] to Hall last year and is a lot better poet, I am confident. But Hall does have some very good qualities, I think, including a certain raciness which will help him be popular. In fact, I think he will be Auden's successor as the idea of a poet, a "popular" sort of poet; at least he seems to me to have the potentialities of becoming such.

Yaddo is one of the places which take in writers for periods such as six weeks—provide them with comfortable living quarters, food, and so on, so that they can write and nothing else. If you want to try for a Yaddo fellowship some time, and could get away from family duties to do it, I'll be glad to try to get one for you, or help. I'd like to go to one myself, but I can't seem to be away from this publishing more than three days at any one time! Yaddo is at Saratoga Springs, New York; MacDowell, similar, is in New Hampshire. On Guggenheims, the committee is changed a good bit each year. They are quite political, I think. Some years, one's particular set of references might really be listened to—another year not so much. Someone such as Louise Bogan would have a lot of influence on the decision most any year, of course. I always felt my name was mud with them and that applicants should not use my name; but this situation has changed a bit in that I have been a reference now for a couple or three successful applications—not because I was on, understand, but my name didn't automatically cross them off, anyway! It's a lousy business, anyway, and I'm rather opposed to the way they do the thing. Lord, it is late, and I can't feel the keys of this machine very well, and I'm not making much sense in rambling on. So I'll stop, always with affection for you.

Cordially,

Alan

LETTERS TO ALLEN TATE

Critic, biographer, poet, novelist, essayist—Allen Tate asserted a strong and lasting influence on the course of American writing during the period when the Swallow press was developing. He lives in Tennessee where he is working on his memoirs.

GUNNISON, COLORADO
July 13, 1943

Mr. Allen Tate
% Kenyon Review
Gambier, Ohio
Dear Mr. Tate:

My agent indicates that a New York publishing house is very definitely interested in seeing an anthology of material selected from the "little" magazines, past and present. I certainly want, of course, to include some of your poems in the anthology. I wonder, then, if you would be so kind as to indicate to me which of the following poems have appeared in such magazines, and which ones:

The Mediterranean
The Cross
Shadow and Shade
The Subway
Ditty

I know that you were familiar with many of the most important "little" magazines during the 1920's and early 1930's, where nowadays one finds it so difficult to fill in gaps in collections. If there was any material in those magazines which offhand you would like to see in such a collection and which I might easily miss, I should be glad if you would suggest it to me.

Like Cleanth Brooks and Red Warren [Robert Penn Warren], under whom I did graduate study and secured a doctor's degree at Louisiana State, I greatly admired your wife's [Caroline Gordon] story "Old Red." But since it appeared in *Scribner's,* I cannot consider it, I am sorry to say. And unfortunately so far I have not in my reading placed my hands on another of her stories which I should like to use. If you have a suggestion there, it also would be much appreciated.

I have never written to you before, and you are likely unfamiliar with my name. I have admired your work very much for a number of years. And I should be glad to have you write to Mr. Brooks or to Mr. Warren about me and my ability to handle this project.

Sincerely,
Alan Swallow

DENVER, COLORADO
December 24, 1957

Dear Allen,

I am writing at this moment to solicit your interest in a journal we have been publishing here called *Twentieth Century Literature: A Scholarly and Critical Journal.* It is a cooperative venture by my former students and me. We are just completing our third volume with the January, 1958, issue.

Our endeavor has been to give good, sound scholarly material on modern literature, articles, bibliography, etc. We have a very important feature in the regular "Current Bibliography" in which we give précis of the periodical materials appearing in the field.

What disturbs me is that the University of Minnesota Library, for some reason, is not a subscriber. When the *United States Quarterly Book Review* was discontinued by the Library of Congress (I was its publisher for the last two years of its life), I transferred many subscriptions to *TCL.* The University of Minnesota Library received three issues of *TCL* of our second volume on this arrangement, but there was no renewal.

I think we have an important, earnest, and valuable publication. I am sending you a sample copy. I hope you will agree that the library there should be a subscriber and will urge that the subscription be taken.

And I hope all goes extremely well for you. Kindest regards of the holiday season.

Cordially,

Alan

P. S. An arrangement has been made for a Japanese translation and publication of a small volume of a selection of 6 or 8 of your essays from *On The Limits of Poetry*. I don't know just how long it will take for it to appear.

DENVER, COLORADO
August 10, 1960

Dear Allen,

Thanks for your note of the 5th. Glad the advance could be of help.

I shall look forward to seeing the review of *The Fathers* [a novel by Tate] in *Encounter*. I think what we are running into here is that "reprints" are treated quite differently from English treatment apparently. Very rarely do they rate regular review space in the big media for review—so rarely that it is a surprise to see one there. I suppose this explains *Time* and possibly *NY Times Book Review*, although the latter is often so slow that one cannot tell yet. They gave one reprint I had, by Janet Lewis, space just like a new book! But this is rare, as I say. Too bad that they don't give such new consideration, as is done in England—a reassessment, as it were. We were more fortunate for space for *Collected Essays* because they could treat it as a *new* book, not a reprint, although, of course, it was very nearly all reprint.

Cecil Day Lewis [then with an English publisher with whom Swallow was negotiating for the reprinting of Tate's work], as you probably know, said even my proposition about the negatives made it too high. I don't understand why at all. Without doubt one day we will be reprinting the book from my negatives, and I could reopen the matter with him once more and give a low price in terms of the fact that two printings could be achieved virtually as one. I have also opened it with Eyre & Spottiswoode on that ground and hope they may say yes. Have written Sir Herbert Read, but in correspondence with his firm (but with another man) about it months ago, which I dug up to refresh my memory, I find that the firm is prejudiced against a book which is not entirely reset. I hope Read himself may overcome that prejudice. We still will make it there, I think.

That *Fathers* [*The Fathers* by Allen Tate, a Swallow Paperbook, 1959] is moving healthfully, I think.

Cordially,

Alan

MARGINAL NOTE: "Robie Macauley at Kenyon had his bookstore order 10 for class use in the fall—paperbound *The Fathers,* I mean. I have been pleased with the sale so far, considering the notice."

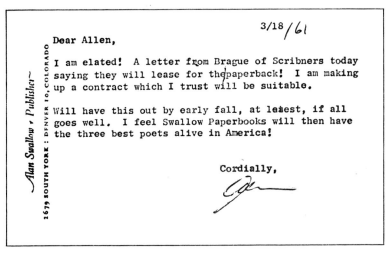

Dear Allen,   3/18/61

I am elated! A letter from Brague of Scribners today saying they will lease for the paperback! I am making up a contract which I trust will be suitable.

Will have this out by early fall, at least, if all goes well. I feel Swallow Paperbooks will then have the three best poets alive in America!

Cordially,

Alan Swallow • Publisher
1679 SOUTH YORK : DENVER 10, COLORADO

DENVER, COLORADO
June 27, 1961

Dear Allen,

I believe you arrive in Wellfleet today. I hope it will be a pleasant summer after a pleasant time in Italy!

I sent the two books you requested, invoice enclosed. Also, I heard from Henry Regnery [of the Chicago publishing firm of that name] and enclose the correspondence. I believe he has come to the correct decision.

One interesting development from my list: I have taken on the full works of Anaïs Nin. This involves publishing a brand new novel (continuing her series of novels and completing it), bringing out a new book of her novelettes, reprinting her stories and her *House of Incest*; then I take over from her one volume in print *Cities of the Interior*. She is aware of our acquaintanceship, I think contacted me because I was publishing *The Fathers* and other works. She sent me to forward to you two former editions of her work, the stories and *House of Incest,* which I will reprint. I am now forwarding these to you. If you have any comment for publicity purposes, it would be welcome!

Her books will all 5 be in print by Sept. 20.

I believe I told you that Scribner had agreed to the Swallow Paperbook *Poems* [by Tate, Swallow Paperbook No. 26], but perhaps the word did not reach you as it came just as you were about to leave. I now have it listed, and I shall have it ready in August. I look forward to it. Lowell Naeve has done me a brilliant cover for it!

Cordially,

Alan

P. S. This fiction business is most interesting. I long maintained that a small publisher should not do fiction, was at a poor situation for it. However, I kept doing some, as I found extremely fine work which was not being done by the large houses. The pace has quickened. And now think what I have accumulated only in about seven years: your *The Fathers,* the good work of Janet Lewis, about 16 novels of Vardis Fisher including his giant Testament of Man series, one of the novels (and perhaps best to date) by the best young novelist in the country, Edward Loomis [probably *The Charcoal Horse,* 1959], a novel by Maude Hutchins, several of Frederick Manfred, the big Minnesota giant, and now all the works of Anaïs Nin. I don't think that, considering the time interval and the quality and the fact of not just reprinting chestnuts of dead authors in new editions, any publisher could match that!

DENVER, COLORADO
November 4, 1964

Dear Allen,

I was pleased to learn today of your appointment to the Poetry selection committee of the NBA. The letter requested sending two possible nominations to you, and I am glad to get them off. They are Jim's [J. V. Cunningham] *To What Strangers, What Welcome* and James Schevill's *The Stalingrad Elegies*.

As you are well aware, it is difficult for the judges to be up to date on all possible titles for the year, inasmuch as several are published late in the year. I am doing a total of eleven books of poetry for 1964 (!) and I think fine [ones] (included is Carol Johnson's, out just recently as you may know), and two more of my titles, I think, are truly "major" titles. But they are late enough that I doubt that the attention of the judges would come to them via reviews. So I am taking the liberty of calling them to your attention.

1. *New and Selected Poems* by Thomas McGrath. Here is a big book, I think. As I remarked in my essays, I feel that he and Lowell are the major developed talents of their particular generation (which happens to be my own, as well). This book just went out for review recently, and I am sending along a copy for your inspection together with the above books.

2. *The Changes* by Samuel French Morse. This is in production and will be issued next month. Clearly, no review attention will be forthcoming in time to catch the end of the year, although it will be published in 1964. So when it is out, with your permission, I will promptly send a copy. It is a big and important book, I am sure.

I hope all goes well and that the recent royalty report was good. Some problems with my leg keep reoccurring, and I am not sure but what I will have to go into the hospital for some major surgery on it—although both the surgeon and I hope still to avoid it. But it has been a problem each year for many months of the year, for quite a number of years now.

Cordially,
Alan

LETTER TO A. H. REITER

A. H. Reiter lives in New York City. At one time he considered distributing books for Swallow. This excerpted letter is part of the correspondence on the contemplated arrangement.

DENVER, COLORADO
April 30, 1958

Dear Reiter,

. . .In your letter, you spoke of differences in our personalities, temperaments. I doubt if you know what mine is, and I don't know what yours is. However, from the comments Vardis Fisher has made about you, and from the evidence of your enthusiasm, and devotion to his work and to the Testament ["Testament of Man," a series of books by Vardis Fisher], you are my friend, too. I would not want to appear to you an old, world-weary, fed-up guy. I am quite energetic and most of the time optimistic—if not philosophically so, that is, convinced of a benign universe, practically so. If I didn't feel that way, I wouldn't have taken on the Testament series. All evidence was that it would be a "failure." But failure to the practices of the New York publishing methods, as I think I tried to explain to you once, does not necessarily mean failure to me. I felt that—when the chips were down and the other publishers couldn't do it—that perhaps my methods would do it. And those are to substitute my own work for much that the New York publisher pays for; I do not have salesmen (that automatically raises the break-even point on a book at least a thousand copies; and Vardis' former publishers proved that the books wouldn't sell that many by their methods); I try to promote, if you will, quietly by conviction and a more "personal" method. If the other would work, the books should be with a New York firm, not with me. If some other publisher can do better with the books, I am doing a disservice to Vardis by publishing them. I would not appear to be merely the hind tit; but this is the game I have made for myself, to publish good books which the New York firms can't seem to publish, for one reason or another.

My publishing was started eighteen years ago. Except for a couple years in the army, I have been at it steadily since. I made my living teaching; I published as a part-time activity, but no less serious because of that. Four years ago I resigned from the University of Denver to work full-time at the publishing because it had grown enough that my family and I thought we could slide by for a time. As a good teacher, I can get a job teaching again when I have to.

So what does this mean? I am not sure—except that I do know a bit about it after 18 years of fighting the battle for books, generally of value, which are not in the popular class. (And just as quickly sending on to New York manuscripts which I felt should be done there because they would be done better than I could do them.) And I know that some of the kinds of promotion you speak of won't materially work. Henry Holt said a generation or more ago that one can spend $5,000 to sell $500 gross value of books, and no truer word has been spoken about publishing. I have tested it a good many times; I have spent $150 for an ad in the *New York Times Book Review* and been able to trace, under reasonably controlled conditions, not a single sale of a book to it. This is just one of many examples. Ads will help, but only for a book that is ready to move or is moving. Other publishers will tell you this, too. And so with so many of the methods of promotion associated with selling. They will work for books, at times. But at others, they are complete and dead losses. When we planned *Jesus Came Again,* we put out quite a bit of money into the circulars, you may remember, mailing lists, informing the booksellers of the change for the series, of the upcoming book, etc. Result? *Goat* sold more than *Jesus* [*A Goat for Azazel* and *Jesus Came Again* are both from "Testament of Man" series], although it did not have any of that promotion. I am not fully able to explain all of such phenomena.

Now about the schools. Both Vardis and I have spent some years in the academic halls. I won't pretend to know all that goes on; indeed, I am startled all the time by movements I see there. But one doesn't haul off and sell a department of sociology or literature upon creating a course for teaching the Testament of Man —particularly when it isn't even finished! We have quite a problem here. It is a problem of selling, but not selling in the high-pressure sense; rather, selling some teachers of English the idea that this series is worthwhile. We meet it among Vardis' former "friends." I know that many of them feel (I had an evidence once again from a man who is a fairly well-known teacher and also an editor of a fairly good little magazine, who said in a letter he had admired Vardis' "early" or "former" work) that Vardis was really on the ball in the thirties, turning out some important novels. But that in his wayward way, he got off the beam when he started the Testament. If they praise Vardis, it is carefully with the qualification that, of course, it was former work, before he committed his big folly. And so on. This is a very long-range matter. We have to sell them the idea that this is important. Vardis and I feel that we are not going to make much headway—that clearly we haven't and the former publishers didn't—until the whole is in and on record. We feel that at that time we can smoke out some of these people. We may still be wrong, but it is the only reasonably immediate hope. We are going to make some of these guys sweat their shoes full. Because it is a full and big and gigantic and great project; but we have little chance of convincing them until they will look at it all. (And we may not be able to make them do it even then, but I think we can.)

Now on Doubleday. I haven't the slightest interest in that firm. The only respect I have for them resides (a) because they publish some books by Fisher; (b) because, although they haven't, I think, earned any money on her, they continue to be willing to publish novels by Janet Lewis [author of *The Wife of Martin Guerre* and others novels and poems]; and (c) because despite their size they still seem more experimental and effective at times than other firms. I don't care if they don't earn a nickel. But I am interested in Fisher, and I am interested in the *Valor* novel, for I think it is a fine one, and I hope it hits the top of all the best-seller lists. Because it has a small chance to make some real money, I think it legitimate, indeed, to move the schedule of the Testament so that there will be no interference at all. In fact, it is just possible the Testament might gain a tiny bit from attention on a more "popular" kind of work. And if I published the same week or possibly even the same month, there is no question but that the review space would go to *Valor,* not to *Satan.*

On the matter of college people, a lot of them in literature, at least, are on my mailing list and receive notices of the Testament series. This is all to the good, although there is no quickly immediate result.

Please believe me that this is in no way an attack on you or upon your ideas. Lordy, without your enthusiasm, the publication of the books would have been more difficult. In truth, if I know anything, it is that I know we can be successful in this only through personal conviction such as you have about it—and my conviction, for I stake quite a bit on it, of time, certainly, as well as some money....By such actions as you have taken—getting this man a bit interested, or that one. . . .Most you have contacted, as you know, have turned away indifferently; but once in a while you have struck a chord. And that is what we have to do. Such actions, such convictions, speak; if you get two, and they get two each in turn; and so on—we can make this Testament into something of considerably wide acclaim.

But if it were as simple as hiring a commission outfit, I'd have the hottest one anywhere in the country. They wouldn't touch it without a guarantee. If a couple thousand dollars in advertising would do it, I'd beg, borrow, or steal it and use it; but it would not sell one hundred books; I'm as certain of that as I am of anything.

No, your other suggestions are the right ones, I think—write the letters, speak to people, get them to act. I'm speaking as loudly as I can in telling the world that I think these books are fine and great, when, apparently, no other publisher will take that stand. And I mention them and talk about them wherever I can. I think that is what we both can do, and all of like mind, and all whom we can make of like mind.

Please be assured of my affection and admiration, and I do count very heavily upon your enthusiasm and help. I wish the selling job were exactly as you conceive it to be.

Cordially,

Alan

LETTER TO NATALIE S. ROBINS

Alan Swallow published two books of poems by Natalie Robins: *My Father Spoke of His Riches* and *Wild Lace*. Swallow Press of Chicago has published a subsequent volume. She lives in New York City, and is the wife of the critic, Christopher Lehman-Haupt.

DENVER, COLORADO
December 3, 1961

Dear Natalie,

Yes, in your new poems, you are showing more power and control and command. I am proud of you. Keep up this way, and you will really be a demanding poet. You are moving more to metre, too, sounding out the power in it. I am sorry that some lines have a slant rhyme instead of a true one; I think this is the one small defect in the whole.

Are you trying magazines now? You should be, consistently and persistently; don't let a few no's floor you. On the whole, you can't be a writer offering without figuring that most editors (even all of them, as a breed) are stupid. So many won't "see" you; but a few will begin to. This is not necessary for book publication, as you already know from *WL* [*Wild Lace*]; but then it can be a help to you, bring in a dollar now and then, and also move you along in other ways.

Very glad you aren't becoming "one of those publishing women." I didn't figure you would.

[Frances] Steloff at Gotham Book Mart and Anaïs Nin cooked up an autographing party at the Gotham for the 7th. They thought of making it a sort of get-together for Swallow authors, although with Nin having the newest things, the attention, I guess, would be mostly on her. I gave her some names. Two of them, you and Thomas McGrath, she could not seem to reach on short notice. I am sorry, but I wish both of you were included. Nonetheless, if you have time that day, drop in and introduce yourself to Nin.

Hope you like her *Seduction* [*Seduction of the Minotaur*].

She and Miller and Durrell were much together in Paris. Both she and Durrell are in *Cancer*. (Have you read *Capricorn*? I really like it better than *Cancer*. Some of his enthusiasts—I started reading him in the late thirties, frankly, but never became quite so adulatory as some—like *Black Spring* best, but I think I like *Capricorn* best. A lot of power and a lot of movement to the prose, versatility with the prose.)

Cordially,

Alan Swallow

LETTER TO MARTIN ROBBINS

Martin Robbins is a poet living in Boston. *Behind the Headlines* is his most recent volume of poetry. He appears frequently in the Boston area on television. He is also a librettist and tenor, and has written for opera. The excerpt below is in response to a suggestion that Swallow hire a local sales representative.

DENVER, COLORADO
March 4, 1965

Dear Marty,

. . .On the salesman situation, I've been up and down that row a lot of times in 25 years of publishing poetry. One won't work there [Boston] in that area, certainly at present; and the books of poetry and the like won't support it, even if the salesman would. In certain spots I have representation on commission basis, but it has to be very choosey to be of any value to the books. To stay in the business I've had to develop techniques outside the methods of the large-scale publishers—which were invented and developed for their books, not these—and they seem to work better than those of the large-scale publisher—on these books, not theirs, of course. This is demonstrated by the fact that I publish with relative success stuff that they couldn't even touch for economic reasons. Sometime, if I find the right sort of person, I might try to work out something again in the area similar to what I have in some other places. In the Los Angeles area I just got rid of one I had, a professional representing some fine New York lines. I had just sold 400 copies of a book in the area, and not one order via him! No, my distribution is the envy of those who try to publish similar work, instead of the other way around.

Cordially,

Alan

LETTERS TO ROGER HECHT

Swallow published Roger Hecht's *27 Poems* in 1966. Another volume of his poems has been published by The Swallow Press, Inc., in Chicago. Mr. Hecht lives in New York City, and has reviewed in leading journals. The three quotations below are excerpts.

DENVER, COLORADO
October 13, 1965

Dear Mr. Hecht,

. . .Thanks for your patience. This is definite acceptance of *27 Poems*. It is a fine book; I am completely convinced and will be proud of it. . .

As for the comments by others, let me see them. I am not too receptive to such things. I have consistently refused to have any introductions to the first books of poetry (although offered by many prominent poets), for I feel that the poet's work must sail forth on its own, and more honestly so. My experience has been that often the poet being published is, in my opinion, better than the introducer; furthermore, that the introduction gets the reviewers, readers, etc., thinking about something else, what the person has said, rather than the poems. And I don't think reputations (except in a popular sense) are made by such. . .

DENVER, COLORADO
September, 1966
(*from a postcard*)

. . .During the past two and a half months, I've made quite a few changes in an effort to get my publishing more manageable once more; it has outgrown my particular methods, yet I am constitutionally opposed to creating an organization. . .

DENVER, COLORADO
November 22, 1966

. . .Don't worry about readings. I think they are probably useful, but it seems to me that there is far more attention on them now than they deserve. Poetic reputations of lasting significance do not, I think, grow out of them.

——————

NOTE: Between the spring of 1965 and the last excerpted letter I've quoted, Alan Swallow sent me a total of nine postcards, six letters, and two royalty statements (both of which included notes). To reread these now, almost a decade after his death, forces me to wonder by what means he was, in these brief and always pointed messages, so uniquely able to convey the wisdom of his experience, his humor, his encouragement, and his absolute refusal to be budged a centimeter from his view of his craft, his desire to remain a small publisher, a small editor. That very word "small," on which he insisted, becomes an irony when one considers that he wrote me he read 250 poetry manuscripts a year and was publishing 65 books per year. He and I were total strangers; yet not once did I feel he was treating me as anything less than a respected author, whereas I was in fact a rude beginner. I am persuaded he gave this sense of casual intimacy and hard-headed practical wisdom to each of his authors. And with these he gave us all—how I don't know—a sense of the dignity of being writers, being involved in a common pursuit, excellence. I have not again encountered his like, and can only hope that the maverick editor-publisher he so well represented shall not vanish. *Roger Hecht.*

LETTER TO RICHARD GILLMAN

His first volume of poetry, *Too Much Alone,* was published by Alan Swallow in the "New Poetry Series," 1965. His poetry has appeared in many periodicals, including *New Poems By American Poets,* Ballantine Books, Inc. In recent years Gillman has been a member of the central administration of the State University of New York.

DENVER, COLORADO
November 2, 1966

Dear Dick,

I have your note of October 27th and hasten with a response, although you did not ask it. I want you to shake loose from any depression because of reviews—or lack of them. *Poetry* is not terribly important. They seem to pass over a great many good books. As I say in an autobiographical piece which will be appearing in *New Mexico Quarterly,* I learned not to pay any real attention to reviews. I feel that I know the work, after all the handling of it I have done, much better than any reviewer. And I bet my judgment against his or against that of the review editor who passes over a book. You are surely familiar with so many examples—that [J. V.] Cunningham was ignored in his first book by the reviewers, that [Yvor] Winters in his books has been typically vilified only to be praised for the same book the next time around, the indifference to Edgar Bowers when first published, etc. In my own case, Dudley Fitts actually said in *Saturday Review* that I wasn't a poet. All I can say is that if you are being ignored in some places you are in the best of company.

Actually, your book has been very well received, indeed. After all, I have published 35 books in the New Poetry Series, and several times that in total books of poems, and I can attest that you have had a reception that is unusually warm.

Cordially,
Alan Swallow

Newsletters

November 12, 1962

from: Alan Swallow
     2679 South York Street, Denver 10, Colorado

Dear Author:

This duplicated letter will contain significant information concerning my publishing; information I will make as brief as possible.

Most persons receiving this will know that when I started publishing, I used a small hand press and handset type for publishing poetry and a little magazine. As the publishing developed over the years, of course printing had to be sought. This was difficult in the West because there was little book manufacturing facility in the entire area. In 1948/49 Mr. Raymond B. Johnson of Boulder, Colorado, came to see me on behalf of Johnson Publishing Company, at that time a new and small printing firm. He indicated to me that he was especially interested in publications printing, something I had hoped to see in the West. Thus began a long association of great value to us both. I was pleased to see his firm grow and grow; I was pleased to be able to advise him, and by marshaling work to help make each feasible, into such steps as adding bookbinding and offset printing to his facilities. In a very short time, indeed, his firm became what is, I believe, the only shop in the mountain area completely equipped to do book manufacturing under one roof, and I have been proud to see that this could be done in the area. The Johnson firm has done in recent years probably more than 90% of my book production, and during those years there were between 30 and 40 books per year being done from my work, plus a considerable amount of magazine printing directly from my work. This relationship was excellent: the Johnson firm was becoming a real asset to the whole region; my own publishing was growing and was holding the work in the region; and the closeness with which we worked together contributed to the situation whereby, I am confident, I was the most productive person in publishing, that is, personally responsible for editorial judgment and production of more titles than any other person in the nation.

The Johnson firm has continued to grow at a most remarkable rate. During this last two years the firm has become so large that it has taken on major, large projects of various types of printing. These were significant and important developments to Mr. Johnson and began to overshadow the various smaller jobs from my work. Inevitably they had to take precedence; my books often were delayed, sometimes to a quite serious extent (as several authors receiving this letter found to their own sorrows). The production had become such that it was no longer so useful nor so efficient in such a plant as Mr. Johnson had admirably built.

The result is that the Johnson firm and I are now separating our close (but always informal, as we neither had investment in the other firm) association. When certain books now in production are completed, they will be the last there; and as of now, any new ones started in production will be done elsewhere.

You will recognize this is a major problem for my work. In a sense, I had almost all my eggs in one basket; now that basket is not there, and there is nowhere in the region another basket. Of course, production is available upon economical and sound basis for my type of work in the Midwest and in the East, and some of this will be used, as it has occasionally in the past. However, I am dedicated to the idea that production facilities should be available in the West, and in association with others, I will aid in the growth of additional facilities in the area. For a time, the book production will have to be in several baskets, to continue the image I have used.

Naturally, this will take more time and attention upon production: it will even take more time per title, since effort will have to be somewhat more scattered among several sources of supply. And some time will have to be taken to planning, a sort of management function about development of production facilities which I hoped to avoid.

Finally, then, this development has its unfortunate, temporary influence of very serious kind upon editorial work. First, since production time per title will be larger and there will be testing of various production facilities, there will be a bit of slow up of immediate schedule. (The editorial problems referred to later have inadvertently aided in that I do not have quite so many manuscripts actually under contract as I had, say, a year ago at this time.) Second, because of the bit more time in production, per title, for this transition period, and also because of the time needed to work at development of production facilities, I will need to cut back temporarily and slightly reduce the number of titles attempted. Third, this needed modification comes at a particularly difficult time because of the manuscript situation which has already developed. The relative "success" of this individualistic and personal publishing, plus the publicity it has received in recent years, has had one big net result, that is, the increase in manuscript submissions. My close estimate is that in this year alone there have been well more than 400 book manuscripts submitted, plus a good many magazine materials. Clearly, it had already got out of hand; I had fallen shamefully behind, not through failure of interest or effort, but really *because* of interest and effort. I am unwilling that my publishing become more than it is, that is, an expression of my judgments about books and talents and values; therefore, the securing of editorial reading is no answer in my eyes.

In a word, I felt strongly that despite the tide of manuscripts and the shameful delays, I was almost holding my own and the good books were appearing and being sold; and in my natural optimism regarding what I can accomplish, I always felt that I would "catch up" and still maintain the same publishing pace, which I have demonstrated that I can maintain both in the amount of work done and also in the economic phase of the publishing. Clearly, with this new situation in production and what will be involved, I can no longer pretend even to myself that I could cover all this work and handle the new problems. It is essential that a good bit of cleaning up be done in order that the problems may be dealt with fully and, in the end, that the ability to publish a large number of good books be maintained. These conclusions seem more than well indicated:

1) All commitments definitely made will be honored. Inas-

much as the manuscript reading had fallen behind because of the pressures indicated (for the difficulties in production have gradually developed, leading to this breaking of the publisher/printer relationship with the Johnson firm), I do not at this moment have so many of these as I had, say, exactly a year ago. Therefore, I have good hope that there will not be, for them, any serious delay, and the schedule planned for them can probably be maintained fairly closely.

2) In selecting new manuscripts for publication, I will naturally provide some preference in reading time for these: (a) those by authors already on my list, as is their due; (b) those authors to whom I have indicated some specific interest. These are sufficient, however, to provide some delays even for those manuscript reports.

3) Certain manuscripts are being returned unread. It would be unfair to hold them at all, especially since some have been here some months. There is no prejudice in such a case; I am sure that among them are several I should like to publish. All I can say to the authors involved is that I am most apologetic, there was no intent on my part that this be the eventuality. Further, if the manuscript is not successfully placed elsewhere and at a later date the author wishes to correspond with me about it, perhaps I can through correspondence help sort out the more "likely" ones and provide a reading upon an efficient basis.

4) Certain manuscripts will be returned upon which I have devoted some, although probably a minimum, of time. I know from that bit of time that I am interested. I cannot in justice do anything now except to return with apology and to say, in effect, "I am interested. I should like an opportunity, if you have not achieved success elsewhere, to have another chance. I will need to solve some of these problems before I could take advantage of a second chance which you might wish to give me. Perhaps an exchange of letters later can determine this."

5) Certain other manuscripts I know I shall wish to do but must be less definite about publication date at this time. Or at least I am inclined, by the work I have done editorially, to this direction. I can only ask of the author in this case: Do you wish

to wait the extended process in view of what has developed, or would you prefer to have your work returned? There will be no prejudice on my part if you wish to try elsewhere while I am working upon these problems; and if you might wish to try again with me later. I can say only if the return is chosen, it would be only fair that upon resubmission, which I would like, I would need, then, to place the script in order with other submissions and provide the preference indicated for materials already somewhat familiar to me.

Cordially yours,

Alan Swallow

October 31, 1963

from: Alan Swallow

2679 South York Street, Denver, Colorado 80210

Dear Author:

A year ago I burdened many of you. . .concerning the problems of production I then faced because of the break with my primary source. I hesitate to burden you with another at this time but do feel it necessary. Most receiving this will know at least an outline or parts of the subsequent events.

1. On Christmas 1962 I suffered a coronary occlusion. Recovery was good in most respects; my schedule since has been kept close to former except that I do much of the work in bed (hence many bad handwritten letters to you); time was seriously lost upon work upon manuscripts (and I am greatly behind even at this time). However the production problems outlined one year ago, serious as they were, were tackled, and by about August 1 the last largish problem seemed to fall into place. As anticipated, this grouping of production methods seems to require a bit more time for most titles; there is more cost involved. However, in 1963 I will be fulfilling, I believe, all commitments made and the total production will be about the same as 1962. I have tried to be more reserved about commitments for 1964 in order to try to cut back the number of titles by 10% or so; the family and friends are after me seriously about watching the energy expenditure. The health problems, further, have remained annoying. Ever since my motorcycle accident of years ago, after the two years of recovery from that,

I had had occasional, chronic difficulties with the leg. But toward the end of April of this year—apparently somehow connected with the coronary and subsequent treatment—the leg erupted into difficult and acute pains, swellings, etc. In the six months since then I have not had even half time relief from this situation. Then during the past two and a half months the situation has remained acute continuously except for approximately two weeks of fair relief. At this moment, after some minor surgery and testing, the doctors may have found something to help and at least promise of relief seems indicated. I mention this because although this has not seriously hampered much of the work, it has hampered that one aspect I prize so much: my own personal printing of the volumes of poetry. Even at that, I believe that by the end of the year I will have printed and published some six volumes of poetry (near the usual average) and one issue of *PS* magazine [a small magazine published by Swallow—*PS* stands for Poems and Stories]. The needs for 1964 will be great, as I hope to have time to indicate.

2. When I went into the paperback business in 1960 (under needs I have spelled out) I started to use Paper Editions Corp., with their warehouses in San Francisco, Los Angeles, Chicago, New York (and later Dallas) as the one "national" wholesaler. Their plan was this: of each title, a "deposit" of copies was made; these were only memo invoiced, that is, they were not to be paid for until that title was closed out (at whatever future date!), only reorders from them were to be paid on 60-day invoice. The discount was 50%. The situation was not good, but it was the only one we had. The pay was slow, almost impossible to get, even upon those 60-day accounts, and by October 1, 1962, I decided I had had enough, particularly after finding precisely the same experience among some other firms. So I withdrew, had all the stock on hand returned (so that I could calculate the sales from Basic Stock (the "deposit")). By the end of the year this was done. The account then dated one year without any payment, for 60-day invoices or for Basic Stock. As soon as I could after the coronary, I wrote severely to the president about it; this was about March 1, 1963. My total amount due from them was approximately

$1,600. At that time, I apparently badgered him into a payment of $500. Within less than a month came the news that PE was in bankruptcy. I was so much better off than many, for most were stuck not only with amounts due but also with loss of that Basic Stock! (one Doubleday man told me two weeks ago Anchor Books was hit very hard by this). I have seen a statement concerning assets, etc., in the bankruptcy proceedings, and there is no hope to recapture even 10% of the amount after years. Therefore, since at least I know exactly how many books they had sold, I am entering them upon royalty reports as sales below cost, not subject to royalty, as the total account of $1,600, even after years, will not net $600, or about 17% of the retail price! If there is an X at this paragraph, your royalty report will have a quantity of paper backs thus indicated.

3. In view of the difficulties of this past year and the effort put out, I am sure that you will agree I am entitled to any relief I can reasonably secure from routines. It has been my practice to carry on semi-annual royalty reports quite some time, shifting to annual slowly. However, the contract permits this either after a time or when royalties are indeed low. If there is an X beside this paragraph, this is indication that I have exercised this option and place your account upon annual report, with all of 1963 reported next March.

4. Briefly: with poetry I am in a real problem; you know my methods to produce myself. By good fortune of the list, in a way, I badly need to raise the number of books done by double. These are no more than the usual number of first volumes, believe me. But a number of people upon my list have matured at the same time with extremely fine 2nd, 3rd, 4th volumes—a really nice result of the work so far! But to do 6 has cost a great deal of energy when it is short. Therefore, I make my first appeal of any kind for help: If you have any equipment to be able to help in production of a book of poems in 1964, let me know. It will be a worthy one, believe me!

October 15, 1965

To my authors and friends:

It has been nearly three years since I composed one of these report/letters. Three years ago this month, I indicated, in one, the problems I faced as a result of breaking off primary relationships with Johnson Publishing Company as basic production supply. Then shortly thereafter, a report about the problems faced after the coronary suffered in December that year. I now wish to bring up to date a report about continuing problems, increasing problems—and some ideas. Despite a tremendous production during these three years, I probably have been successful in increasing problems rather than decreasing them.

First, about production: For basic work, I have been using the World Press of Denver; this small firm was letterpress only; to a large extent, the plant was double-shifted to take care of my needs. In order to secure offset production adequately, I did three things: one small offset press was leased and then subleased—to a succession of three persons who have run it part-time for my work; this was a press with which we had experimented just before my coronary with some thought of setting up a small production shop in Taos, a plan which fell through. Second, I secured a smaller offset machine (recently traded in for one of the same size but better) to put with my old letterpress clumper in the shop here for work I could do. Third, since World Press had space but no offset facility, I entered into partnership with Mr. Lou Doughty of World Press (our firm known as Yorkridge Press) to buy a medium-sized press, later augmented with camera; and this press has worked primarily on my work. The binding is done separately. Thus, although there is not the facility of doing work under one roof any more, it is close at hand and has worked quite well. Occasional work is still done by others, particularly in rerun of offset plates either in Ann Arbor or with Johnson—where the plates had first been run.

Second, about health: The recovery from the coronary has been quite usual and good, I think. The cardiograms show good results; I am, of course, on the usual routine of anti-cholesterol and anti-coagulants, augmented with some other pills; my doctor seems to go along with this type of regime, fairly common today. With my work load and incessant hours, I suppose there is some concern; but when I can keep to the regimen closely, even with rather little sleep, I feel good, and the signs of distress, such as angina pain, are small. The real difficulty came about five months after the coronary, when pain and swelling came to my damaged leg. It has been a relatively continuous problem since. It took many, many months of treatment, various antibiotics, etc., before the diagnosis seemed clear; in fact, I had one night sterilized a razor blade and opened myself one eruption which gave us our first clear test of the infection, despite an earlier bit of surgery to find out. It is clear that sometime during the three bouts of surgery I had with the leg after it was smashed, I contracted hospital staph, as it is known—osteomyelitis (I am not sure of the spelling at the moment) of the bone. It is over quite an extensive area—some 8 or 9 inches long; the blood supply there is poor because it is of the bone and also because of the old scar tissue. Therefore, even if a good antibiotic were found (and we have tried all the doctor thinks I can safely take—and for a year and a half I have had antibiotics at least 2/3 of the time), it is not expected, now, that it can get well enough to the infection to destroy it. I am currently on a long trial of one relatively new one which I had tried briefly last spring and could not tolerate but am tolerating now. But none of us has any real hope for it. The pattern was that I would have an acute attack from the infection —tremendous pain (and only an awkward type of painkiller to use safely), swelling, etc., for a period of four to six weeks, with antibiotic; then the infection would move to one particular spot, find a chance to get out, and there would be relief from pain as it seemed to die down; then perhaps four weeks or so of quiescence, and then attack again. Last New Year's Day, when this happened, I resolved to go on the crutches again to relieve the pain of use of the leg and have remained on them ever since (except violations through impatience or pressure of work to be done, too frequent, I am sure). They have helped by seeming to spread out the attacks. After debates, resolving one way and then another, it now seems fairly clear that I will have to have surgery in an effort to take out enough of the bone to hope to get rid of this. I have resisted this about as long as I can, and if the current antibiotic does not help a great deal, this will probably be scheduled for sometime in the early part of next year.

My recounting of this is merely to indicate that the health problems themselves help point up another matter: that is the general work load I have imposed upon myself, and the consequences of this work load. Inasmuch as I had to secure help for the shipping itself, I had more energy and time for production and editorial work—at least at first. So the production built up to what may seem to be the stupid level of fifty books a year last year—and likely the same for 1965. Handling this side myself, you can imagine having twenty titles in various stages of production at once and some new title appearing on the average of nearly once a week! For a time, I could handle it. And then the difficulties arose. The health, in part, yes; but much more: first, the shipping. Of the boys I have had doing this, the first and third were excellent: efficient, quick, willing to take responsibility and see it was done right, taking an interest in some stock control, and above all, perhaps, being considerate of me and trying to save me steps. The third one left in June, and since then the shipping has been very close to a shambles. . . .

I have been compelled, in order to keep it moving at all, to spend hours per day—a total of many, many hours per week— right in the shop in some sense helping, training, often working without the crutches and with some acute stages of the attacks. So the other work has suffered badly, badly, and I have felt rather desperate about it. I am to start training another boy toward the end of November, having two to work during Christmas rush, and I shall dearly hope that this time I shall have a good one. Second, the pressure of manuscripts. I don't really know at times how to cope with this. I resolved to try to handle, as intelligently as I can, 400 book mss. a year. But the number coming unannounced or queries began to double this. Just to write letters saying that manuscripts shouldn't be sent requires a lot of time per week, let alone handling others; and even the poor ones, to get a note done, then package, etc., takes a good deal of time each, no matter how impossible they are for me. The result is that I have been quite dissatisfied with my own work—at least a good deal of it—editorially during the last year or so. It isn't as good as it was or should be; and I mean primarily in getting my deepest attitudes developed about a project, being cooperative and helpful in developing potentials I could see in work, and that sort of thing.

I'll use this as an example: Vardis Fisher and Opal were here in Denver a week end three weeks ago, a very enjoyable time. However, they saw me in one of those periods that I now name for a phrase Vardis used. He said I had gone completely gray. I do suffer from these occasionally, in that period for several nights running—the vitality knocked completely down, a "grayness," perhaps is the best way of saying it. This is only temporary; I assure you that I feel vigorous and am vigorous most of the time. But: Vardis "read the riot act" to me then, in accord with what many have told me, including my family. I must find some way of resolving some of these pressures, no matter how self-imposed they have been in their origins. There might be some ways of doing this, although with some difficulty. One of them is to cut the number of new titles; and I promised at that time to Vardis and to my family that I would cut back the number of titles in 1966. (I'll be candid to admit that this would be a natural result, for the shambles of shipping in recent months has meant even less editorial work, so that I really don't have so many projects planned!)

What Vardis failed to recognize fully is that I had made an effort to solve the problem. A year ago a young man (who had been about the place several times, chatting, observing what was going on) came and asked to be apprenticed to me, with a view toward possible entrance into the firm by investment, etc. So we developed a plan for a two-year apprenticeship while he was finishing his B.A. (this last spring) and possibly doing graduate work. At the end of the period, if all looked well and agreeable on all sides, I would incorporate and the portion decided upon would be sold to him and he would come into the work fully. I taught him to print both letterpress and offset, some other aspects of the work; the program was to stretch across each side of the work step by step. However, last month I decided that he was not the person for it. This is not a criticism of the young man; he is a person with many, many qualities; but he did not seem the right one to me. (Undoubtedly, this will be very difficult to find, for I am probably a difficult person in this matter.) Now consider this: I had thought I had taken a very good step forward in doing exactly what all have advised: if it would have worked well, it would have been ideal—in splitting labor gradually, in promising to maintain the future no matter what happened to me, and so on. But it didn't: and although the young man, indeed, did a good deal of work for me, I of course spent hours and hours of time and a tremendous amount of energy (taken from my other work) to train with this hope for the final result. So, I say to Vardis and others, I tried what seemed a good plan! In that sense, it set me back a year in getting at the problem—although, understand, not a year lost.

I shall have to tackle it another way. Yes, cutting back some titles will help and will permit me to get caught up a bit more; if I can get a good shipping boy again, I shall have more relief. But "cutting back" is not so easy as it sounds, and not so advisable as it sounds on the surface. I have many obligations to authors, and to my mind, at least it is important to fulfill them insofar as I can —as a person of large energy, I can do much. But some thought of selling one aspect of the work (say, the Sage Books imprint alone; or some other split). To find the person interested, to keep away from the capitalization (I built my capital by work, you see) which would exact its tribute from the sales as well as trying to earn a salary type return—this publishing just should not be saddled with such; it would destroy its central being. So perhaps I shall have to find a person who can do the work but earn part living elsewhere while gradually taking ownership of a section through earnings from publishing. I may not be clear in my statement, but I hope I am, for it is pretty clear in my mind. Something of that sort may work.

Of course I could sell part or all; there are values worth "buying," if someone wanted them merely to exploit them for a return and let much go by. But so far I have turned aside even the smallest approaches of that kind and will continue to do so. I would rather see it dispersed in another way than to have that happen.

At least, here are some of my thoughts as of this once-in-three-years report!
Alan Swallow

TWENTY-FIVE: an occasional free commentary/publicity leaflet issued from Alan Swallow, Publisher

from 2679 So. York, Denver, Colorado 80210

Number Two: Dated February 1, 1966

Number One of this leaflet promised two matters which should
probably be taken care of immediately with the next issue, Number Two.

1. I indicated then (October 1, 1965) that there would be an announcement of plans for the start of publication of Anaïs Nin's
Diary in a joint imprint with a large New York firm. That announcement is ready: In April will appear the first volume under
the title *The Diary of Anaïs Nin: 1931-1934.* The editor is Gunther
Stuhlmann, with an introduction; and there will be some illustrations. The publishing imprint will be The Swallow Press and
Harcourt, Brace & World. The price is expected to be $6.95. Al-
though Harcourt, Brace & World will do the basic merchandising
of this volume for the joint imprint, I will be glad to carry some
copies here for those who desire to secure them here. This volume
covers the years in Paris, with many persons involved: Henry
Miller, Antonin Artaud, Dr. Otto Rank, etc.

We will be expecting to carry on the publication of the *Diary*
in many volumes, the second already being in an editing process
at this time. Ultimately, it will be hoped to have this immense
work into print entirely.

2. I indicated that I would give a brief table of chronology of my
publishing. This I will make as schematic as possible.

School year 1939-40. During that fall I borrowed $100 from
my father and purchased a second-hand 5 x 8 Kelsey hand press
(which I still have as keepsake; several persons have borrowed
this and used it at times), some type and furniture. I taught myself to print—and some history of printing and typography—from
books and in practice of issuing two volumes in simple paper
covers: *Signets: An Anthology of Beginnings,* ed. Brantley and
Shorey, composed of poems, stories, and artwork done by students
who had assembled at Baton Rouge, primarily studying with
Cleanth Brooks and Robert Penn Warren. This volume was done

about March, 1940, and was the first to carry a Swallow imprint. The second, the first volume of Swallow Pamphlets, for *First Manifesto* by Thomas McGrath, and it appeared about April, 1940. This was my last full school year in graduate study (I left, of course, with the usual situation: all done except the dissertation, which I completed and handed in for the degree in 1941). I did not consider these first two efforts as trade books. With the type worn and this experience, and with consultation of a typographer friend. . .I secured some new type and thought I was ready to begin in earnest.

School year 1940-41. During the summer of 1940, in Powell, Wyoming, I started the work handsetting and printing the first full volume of poems, *In Plato's Garden* by Lincoln Fitzell. I have always thought of this as one of my best efforts in printing. It was finished and published in the fall of 1940 in Albuquerque, where I had gone to teach at the University of New Mexico. I consider it my first trade book. That fall and on into the school year I started the magazine *Modern Verse* (to last one year until combined with *New Mexico Quarterly Review* when I became poetry editor of that journal), did more Swallow Pamphlets. During that school year I met Mr. Horace Critchlow, a graduate student, who was interested and supplied capital for buying out a small job printing outfit which had been run part-time from a man's basement.

1941-42. We published in Albuquerque under the imprint Swallow & Critchlow. We did miscellaneous printing to support the work, and at that time the name Big Mountain Press was developed as the name of the printing facility. Also, branching out a bit, the name Sage Books was first used (although not considered a separate imprint at the time) to indicate a series of paperbound books of regional interest: *Three Spanish American Poets* and *Rocky Mountain Stories,* ed. by Ray B. West, Jr. In early 1942, Critchlow was called to the army, we dissolved our partnership, he took the larger equipment; I took the titles, inasmuch as I knew I would be going on with publishing, and my original type and handpress.

School year 1942-43. That year I moved to Gunnison, Colorado, to teach at Western State College of Colorado. During that year, on the handpress and through some hired printing, several more volumes of poetry and of the Swallow Pamphlets appeared. These had returned to the Alan Swallow imprint.

October 1943 to December 1945, I was in the Army. I issued no new volumes although I remained active as poetry editor of *New Mexico Quarterly Review;* it is possible there may be a title or two with the Alan Swallow imprint of those years.

Denver: I moved to Denver to teach at the University of Denver in January, 1946. I immediately started in publishing again, and this is a schematic outline of the multifaceted work:

ALAN SWALLOW IMPRINT. This was begun immediately, of course. It has remained the primary imprint for literary materials continuously since that time. This, of course, has moved from a primary interest in poetry to include fiction, literary criticism, literary bibliography, etc.

THE SWALLOW PRESS IMPRINT. Many persons call my work The Swallow Press; but it is to be noted that this imprint has been used only in conjunction with a joint-imprint arrangement with some other firm. I had come out of the Army with some ideas of how a small, literary publisher might cooperate successfully with a large, commercial firm. I sent out this plan, and William Morrow & Company (Thayer Hobson, of fine memory, was president of Morrow then) was the first to take up the idea. Arrangements were concluded in May of 1946 (arrangements which helped determine, incidentally, that I would remain in Denver), and in 1947 the first titles of the joint imprint The Swallow Press and William Morrow and Company appeared. From then until 1951 some 20 titles or so appeared. In 1951 Morrow and I concluded, in a most friendly fashion, that this arrangement was not doing for either of us exactly what we had hoped; so the joint imprint was abandoned, and I moved to Denver the titles that were then in print; as the years went by and any were reprinted, they were of course moved to the Alan Swallow imprint. The Swallow Press imprint was used jointly also on one occasion with the University of Denver Press, and, now, as indicated overleaf, it is being used in joint effort with Harcourt, Brace & World, Inc.

SAGE BOOKS. When I arrived in Denver, I found that Mr. Critchlow had come here, also. He still was interested in publishing. I had already begun work again with the AS imprint and had the plans for joint work with a New York firm. Critchlow had moved to Denver, also, that printing equipment which had been used in the Swallow & Critchlow endeavors for about a year in Albuquerque. We decided that an interesting field of pioneering in publishing would be books about the West; so in 1947 Sage Books was formed as a corporation, technically, although it worked as a partnership. It remained in this status (we used Mr. Critchlow's address to keep matters separate from the AS endeavors) and did, indeed, do primary pioneering in the regional field until 1953, when Mr. Critchlow decided to move to California. At that time, the corporation was dissolved; the imprint Sage Books became a sub-imprint of the over-all effort of Alan Swallow, Publisher; and I sold out the titles involved in the corporation's effort. These titles added to the stock I had to promote at about the time matters seemed to conjoin, as related below.

UNIVERSITY OF DENVER PRESS. In 1946-47, I was encouraged by the head of the English Department at Denver University and by the graduate dean to make some proposals for establishing a university press. I consulted two other men in this, and we made a report which became the basis for establishing the Press, of which I was director during its existence; the beginning was in 1947; in 1953 I asked to return to full-time teaching (I had taught those years two-thirds time and directed the Press one-third time), but early in the fall of 1953 the decision had been reached to abandon the University of Denver Press because of the then financial emergencies of the University. So although I picked up full-time teaching, in the school year 1953-54, I oversaw the disposition of the Press titles. This has pertinence to my own publishing only in that I believed in many of these titles and, not getting suitable offers elsewhere, I borrowed some money and through some long-term arrangements with the University, secured a number of them for the Alan Swallow and Sage Books imprints.

AUTHOR AND JOURNALIST. Three men secured this famous old magazine on the death of Mrs. Bartlett, and in return for a small portion of stock and some badly-needed space, I edited the magazine for two years, about 1951-53. There, we did a few book titles in the field of how to write. When the magazine was sold to Nelson A. Crawford, he did not wish the books; so I took them over and finished selling them out.

During this period, also, the contract to publish *United States Quarterly Book Review* for the Library of Congress provided the first real income for us to take from publishing and led to the building of a garage-type structure on the back of our home lot which provided the basis for shipping, presses, etc., necessary for operating the larger effort. Matters had so moved that titles from my efforts had gathered from many places (the continuous effort of the Alan Swallow imprint at all times; the titles brought from New York with dissolution of the Swallow Press and William Morrow effort; the titles I secured from the University of Denver Press effort; the titles (now all gone) from Sage Books, Inc., as that imprint became solely subsidiary; and a few titles from A & J (now also gone) and in 1953-54 I had an over-all catalogue for the first time in TLA. Actually, there was a cooperative catalogue in TLA with a couple other presses for two or three years; but when all of these titles mentioned had been put together by 1954, they made a substantial backlist, perhaps showing some unity in such multifarious activity of nearly a decade and a half. Big Mountain Press has revived to do production for others under sponsorship of A & J, and that became a sub-imprint, also, during this period. Thus, with all this brought together and requiring much work, and the foundation thus set up, I resigned from the University of Denver (effective August, 1954) and went full-time into the publishing.

The effort has, then, concentrated upon the Alan Swallow imprint for its field (Swallow Paperbooks joining it about 1960); Sage Books imprint for its demarked field (Western Sage Paperbooks joining it about 1960 or 1961); Big Mountain Press for production and marketing service to institutions and individuals; and, just now, revival of Swallow Press imprint in its joint work with another publisher.

The Three Hands of Alan Swallow

THE THREE HANDS OF ALAN SWALLOW   James Schevill

Poet, playwright and teacher, James Schevill was closely associated with the development of poetry in the San Francisco Bay
area. He is now on the faculty of Brown University. Schevill was
among the early Swallow authors. Among his books are *Selected
Poems: 1945-1959, Private Dooms and Public Destinations: Poems
1945-1962,* and *The Buddhist Car and Other Characters.* He has
published six volumes of plays and two biographies.

In a letter to me in 1963 Swallow wrote after a heart attack:
"I have had, of course, the normal concerns about the heart, and
the additional problems that a three-handed guy feels when he
has to work with two hands now." Somehow, with the many obligations that he felt in the world of books, he was never able to
cut back his work to two hands and remained three-handed until
his untimely death in November, 1966. The three hands of Swallow might be called his own poetry, his teaching and criticism, and
his publishing. Many people think of him only as a publisher, but
without his other preoccupations he would never have developed
the unique sensibility and integrity that characterized his career
in publishing.

The body of his poetry is small. Most of the poems that he
wanted to retain are in his book, *The Nameless Sight: Poems 1937-
1956,* published by The Prairie Press in Iowa City. His style was
mainly traditional, influenced by such poets and friends as Yvor
Winters, Robert Penn Warren (with whom he studied at Louisiana State University) and J. V. Cunningham. Since he was also
the publisher of Winters and Cunningham, it was natural that he
should have their classical, critical standards in mind—direct,
rational statement, lines stripped to the bone, the formal poem
that at its best reverberates with the proud clarity of sensitive perception. In a fine poem, "Four Notes on Love," he wrote:

> Love is experience—
> That place we always lose

But always gain with sense.
Whatever flows is gone, but the flow.
In me that flow delivers love.

Always this flow of experience and love is evident in his work. A humility and warmth permeate Swallow's poetry that put the mighty ego of other poets to shame. In a long poem, "Series for My Friends," written after his discharge from the Army in 1945, he wrote his praise of the many modern poets whose work he admired, and then ended:

. . .And I, who read and printed words,
Work warm within that marvelous air.
Return? The soldier turns to the home
To find it moved; and walks, like poets,
Unguarded through the trees.

Always he lived and worked "warm within that marvelous air," yet, as a poet, he knew that he walked always "unguarded through the trees." (Not that he didn't admire the machine too; he was a furious driver of fast cars; owned four at one point, and was devoted to motorcycles too until he suffered a bad accident.) This poetic dedication gave him the courage finally to leave the relative security of the teaching profession and, despite the financial risk, devote himself to publishing.

His teaching and criticism were remarkable in that they denied and avoided the sense of closet scholarship that marks our time. He remained dedicated always to the life of the work. In one sense, Swallow was closely associated with the "New Criticism." He studied with Cleanth Brooks and Robert Penn Warren. He knew and admired such writers as Allen Tate, John Crowe Ransom, and particularly Yvor Winters with whom he had such a close and valuable relationship as friend and publisher. Swallow took from the best of the New Criticism its primary devotion to the text, its attempt to break through sentimental reflections about the author to the elements of the work. But, unlike some of the New Critics, he never fell into the fatal trap of dissecting the poem mercilessly and leaving it in pieces. Perhaps this was because of Swallow's continuous liberal, humanistic concerns. For him the poem was never cold, pure and abstract, but a mysterious product of man's "nameless sight," as he called his own book of poems so aptly. In academic and social concerns too, during the savage attacks of the McCarthy era, he proved his devotion to civil rights and to academic freedom and provided a model of conduct which his students could only admire. Another important point separated him from many of the New Critics—his concern for artistic experiments of all kinds. In a symposium on "Experimental Poetry" that he edited for *The New Mexico Quarterly Review* in 1946, he wrote:

Experimentalism in poetry, then, is evidently a "real" thing. Our most inclusive account of its methods in the modern period is that of Yvor Winters under his terms "primitivism" and "decadence." But there is a place for a more inclusive term historically and categorically, and that term, apparently is to be "experimental." The term refers to two matters, so far as I can judge:

(1) Historically it refers to efforts to create new methodologies, new technical resources for perception and communication, and to the critical test of these in the trial-and-error "laboratory" of writing a poem.

(2) In the modern period, this inclusive meaning of the term has not fully been realized. In most cases it has referred to excerpting from the tradition, isolating certain resources of poetry and extending them into a new context. This experimental effort has been justified in criticism by a feeling that the matter of modern life required certain techniques to handle it; that the poet has been isolated by the *bourgeoisie* and must investigate the unsullied realm left to him; that the impact of science and loss of faith had fractured the experience and created the dissociated sensibility. Whatever the drive or rationalization, modern experimentalism has netted us possibly a very few new techniques of carry-over value to later generations. But it has netted us some very fine poems—undoubtedly several great poems—which are of the sort which investigate one corner of our experience with great ability; to say it another way, in these poems we have a remarkable and permanent record of the dissociated sensibility.

This justification of experimentalism is characteristic of Swallow's critical objectivity that enabled him to influence so many students and writers. If he himself by training was basically in sympathy with the kind of experimentation that functions within the framework of traditional forms, instead of exploding and changing these forms completely, he was nevertheless open to any new development with genuine individuality that was not merely sensational. This was the primary reason why he was able to develop such a wide-ranging list of authors in his efforts as a publisher.

Publishers who are dedicated to books (as apart from those publishers who produce books mainly as commercial products) can be divided into two distinct categories—the man with finely tuned eyes and fingers, who feels and looks at all aspects of the book from cover and type to illustrations and content, and the man who is chiefly concerned with the book as the right kind of reading material, the book as a central part of the cultural process. The first publisher is a dedicated aesthete—a book literally feeds all his senses. He tends to speak only of the fine art of printing and his finest books tend to end up in collections, museums or rare book sections of libraries. The second publisher is an idealist of the word. To him the printed language is supreme, a way to pass on high standards, to maintain traditions, to continue the heritage of humanity. Alan Swallow was such an idealist of the word. Sometimes the books he published tended to be rather plain in appearance. He could never completely solve the financial and equipment problems that would have enabled him to produce fine editions. He published many books that were attractive in appearance, but the fact is that he was more concerned with publishing a variety of important work than with the way each book appeared. As for illustrations, in 1964 Swallow wrote to the artist, Leonard Breger, who illustrated my long poem about the Battle of Stalingrad, *The Stalingrad Elegies:*

As for poetry illustrations, I am one who believes that this is a bastard art and should not be used very often. But, occasionally, it can be very effective—as it was in the job you did for *The Stalingrad Elegies.* I was happy about it, the compliments on the book have been many...But in a book of lyrics, meditative poems, etc., that are most customary, I can't conceive of illustration. How would one illustrate, for example, Frost's great poem, "Desert Places"?

This quotation reveals Swallow's concern for the supremacy of the word and his caution about the relationships of literature with other arts. He was too deeply involved in the battle for an independent American literature to worry much about the growing specialization of the arts which, in many ways, was only a reflection of the vast specialization in the sciences. His concern was for a literature that would again reflect the stubborn independence and taste of one man, not the anonymous compromise of committees that increasingly controlled the magazines and publishing houses. As one of the few independent publishers who was free to publish his own taste, he ignored the difficulties of distribution and neglect that he faced in the commercial book world. Particularly, since he did not advertise his books in the usual way through newspapers and magazines, he faced the difficult problem of getting his books reviewed. It is a tribute to his reputation that, gradually, most of his books were widely reviewed despite his refusal to use the customary methods of advertising and promotion. In the end he achieved an extraordinary variety of publication which is only beginning to be appreciated. A short listing of some of his books illustrates the remarkable range of his work.

The fiction he published included the fine historical novels of Janet Lewis; the work of Vardis Fisher; the moving Indian novel, *The Man Who Killed The Deer,* by Frank Waters; an unusual satirical comic novella, *Memoirs of a Natural-Born Expatriate,* by Richard McBride; and the distinguished experimental books of Anaïs Nin. Under the imprint of Sage Books, he published many outstanding volumes of Western Americana. He earned a place of honor for leading writers in this field with such important books as *Masked Gods* by Frank Waters, *Montana Pay Dirt: A Guide to the Mining Camps of the Treasure State* by Muriel Sibell Wolle and *Boom Towns of the Great Basin* by Frank C. Robertson and Beth Kay Harris.

Still it was in poetry, his own gift and desire, that he most affected the craft of publishing. Where most New York publishers proved their indifference to poetry by publishing only two or three volumes a year and complaining of financial losses, Swallow in his last years was publishing ten or more volumes of poetry a year and making a small profit above expenses. In addition to

Yvor Winters, Allen Tate, J. V. Cunningham, Lincoln Fitzell and Howard Baker, he printed many younger poets such as Thomas McGrath, Harvey Shapiro, Bert Meyers, Gene Frumkin, Eve Triem, Ann Stanford, Edgar Bowers and Alan Stephens. An example of the unusual and moving sense of responsibility that Swallow had toward poetry was his publication of Lucille M. Nixon's and Tomoe Tana's collection of Japanese-American Tanka, *Sounds from the Unknown*. Who else would have published a volume written by hundreds of Japanese-Americans all over the United States? Another little-known example of Swallow's dedication to poetry was his series of *Books on the Renaissance* which emphasized the achievements of various unrecognized poets of that period. Swallow's generosity and integrity in the publishing of poetry earned him the following tribute from James Dickey in *Poetry*, February, 1964: "How many poets—superb ones, half-good ones, promising ones—must go to sleep each night of their lives murmuring, 'Thank the Lord for Alan Swallow.' Though my connection with the Swallow press is limited only to reading, reviewing, and in general admiring its products, I wish to add my thanks also."

As a poet and playwright, I am one of those writers who went to sleep praising Swallow. He published and supported my poetry at a time when I needed support and went on even to publish a volume of my plays though he was not particularly concerned with drama. At the time of his death we were planning a new volume of my poetry and a reprint of my biography of Sherwood Anderson which he had originally published when he was editor of the University of Denver Press. Looking back at my association with Swallow, I know that he taught me an invaluable lesson about life and literature in this country. They are inseparable and each one of us is responsible for the connections we make between our daily lives and the spirit of imagination that creates the value of the printed page. The example of his integrity made it impossible for anyone connected with him not to recognize the dangers and the hopes of literature in this strangely powerful and chaotic society. In the early 1950's when I was editing a little magazine in newspaper format called *Berkeley*, Swallow wrote for me an article, "Directions in Publishing," which still reverberates with the truth of his insights:

> . . .Both the short-range and the long-range conditions for publishing are deeply, deeply disturbing. It is hardly possible to think that our literature will be defeated by complete commercialization into the cheap and shoddy, or that, in another long-range development, 'serious' books would need to be charitably 'sponsored' and the commercial publisher deteriorate to the level of the commercial magazines; yet, like atomic warfare, conditions for this grisly prospect confront us each day as we go to our literary labors. . .

> What will be left? After the volatile stuff is gone, remains the more permanent ash, and I believe my readers will join me in thinking these the best books of all. So long as the price-cost situation is so terribly critical for these books, we must strive through any efforts we can make—choosy buying of books, encouragement to non-commercial publishers, even direct individual help to see that good books get published when they have little other chance. However small it is —and it must seem appallingly small in the strait we have entered— each person must help in his own measure. I wish that I might relieve him of his responsibilities and say that some man, somewhere, will right all the wrong and lead us into the meadow of a great future literature, recognized as it deserves; but each of us is that person.

As Swallow predicted, the commercial publishers face increasingly the danger of deteriorating "to the level of commercial magazines." Yet the solution remains: *each of us is that person.* Only the extraordinary imagination, integrity, and energy of individuals will save us—like the three hands of Alan Swallow.

A SHORT BIBLIOGRAPHIC NOTE

on Alan Swallow, with a selected checklist of books written or
edited by Swallow. The 1966 book list issued by Alan Swallow,
Publisher, is appended.

Alan Swallow was born on February 11, 1915, in Powell,
Wyoming, and graduated from Powell High School in 1932. He
received the bachelor's degree from the University of Wyoming
in 1937, and the M.A. and Ph.D. degrees from the Louisiana State
University in Baton Rouge in 1939 and 1941, respectively. At LSU
he studied under the novelist, critic and poet, Robert Penn Warren.

After receiving his doctorate, Swallow joined the faculty at
the University of New Mexico. It was in Albuquerque that he
became associated with Horace Critchlow and where he published his first book: a volume of poetry by Lincoln Fitzell in a
limited edition handbound by Hazel Dreis of Santa Fe.

Prior to entering the U. S. Army in 1943, Swallow taught
English at Western State College, Gunnison, Colorado. He received
a medical discharge in 1945 and moved to Denver. There he
became an associate professor at Denver University and head of
the creative writing program. From 1947 to 1953 he also directed
the University of Denver Press. In 1954 he left the University to
devote full time to his own publishing enterprises.

His major imprint was Alan Swallow, Publisher, but there
were several others, for example: Sage Books, Big Mountain Press,
Swallow Paperbooks.

In 1947 he received a postwar creative writing fellowship
from the Rockefeller Foundation. He was chairman of the Colorado branch of the American Civil Liberties Union in 1952, and
president of the Colorado Authors League in 1958-59. Swallow
was an active participant in cultural affairs in the Denver area.

He married Mae Elder in 1936 and they had one daughter,
Karen.

Alan Swallow died on Thanksgiving Day 1966 in his Denver
home at the age of 51.

BOOKS BY ALAN SWALLOW

XI Poems. Prairie Press, Iowa, 1943.

The Remembered Land, poems. The Press of James Decker, Illinois, 1946.

The War Poems of Alan Swallow. Fine Editions Press, N.Y., 1948.

The Nameless Sight, Poems 1937-1956. Prairie Press, Iowa, 1956.

An Editor's Essays of Two Decades, criticism. Experiment Press, Seattle and Denver, 1962.

Swallow edited some fifteen books during his career including *The Rinehart Book of Verse,* 1952, reissued by Holt, Rinehart and Winston, 1962. He edited other anthologies including *Anchor in the Sea: An Anthology of Psychological Fiction,* published first by Alan Swallow, Publisher, then by William Morrow & Co. in 1947, and reissued several times since.

A good checklist of the writing of Alan Swallow including his work as a poet and critic, together with a list of articles and reviews about Swallow, appeared in *The University of Denver Quarterly,* Volume 2, Number 1, Spring, 1967, by Dennis D. North. The major portion of the issue is a memorial tribute to Swallow. There are contributions by Mark Harris, Thomas McGrath, Anáis Nin, Edgar Bowers, Frank Waters, Donald F. Drummond, Frederick Manfred, Robert Penn Warren and others.

Scholars and others interested in Alan Swallow's career will want to read "Alan Swallow, Publisher, 1915-1966," by Norma N. Yueh, which appeared in *The Library Quarterly,* Volume 39, Number 3, July 1969.

1966 BOOK LIST OF ALAN SWALLOW, PUBLISHER

This listing appears to contain all of the Swallow titles in print at the time of his death. No effort has been made to correct some obvious inconsistencies in the citations. The abbreviations shown in the heading are: SB—Sage Books, WSP—Western Sage Paperbooks, BP —Bancroft Booklets.

Allen, Catherine Ward, and Harry E. Chrisman, Chariot of the Sun. 1964 SB NF $4.75

Allen, Evelyn L., Sarah Ropes, Eizenija Shera, Index to Little Magazines 1964-65. 1966. $7.50

Ames, Bernice, Antelope Bread, 1966 P $3.00

Back, Joe, Horses, Hitches and Rocky Trails. 1959 SB NF $2.75

——The Sucker's Teeth. 1965 SB F $2.95

Bain, William E., B&O in the Civil War. 1966 SB $5.00

——Frisco Folks. 1961 SB NF $5.00; WSP $2.00

Baird, Donald. See Bell, Inglis

Baker, Howard, Ode to the Sea and Other Poems. 1966 P $3.50

Baker, James Rupert, ed., Poems of Henry King. Books of the Renaissance Series. 1960 P $3.00

Bancroft, Caroline, Augusta Tabor: Her Side of the Scandal. 1955 BP NF .75

——The Brown Palace in Denver. 1955 BP NF .75

——Colorful Colorado. 1959 NF, BP, $2.00

——Colorado's Lost Gold Mines and Buried Treasure. 1961 BP NF $1.25

——Denver's Lively Past, 1959 BP NF $1.00

——Famous Aspen. 1954 BP NF $1.00

——Glenwood's Early Glamor. 1958 BP NF .75

——Gulch of Gold: The History of Central City, Colorado, SB NF $6.00

——Historic Central City. 1951 BP NF .85

——Silver Queen: The Fabulous Story of Baby Doe Tabor. 1953 BP NF $1.50

——Six Racy Madams of Colorado. 1965 BP NF $1.50

——Tabor's Matchless Mine and Lusty Leadville. 1960 BP NF .75

——Unique Ghost Towns and Mountain Spots. 1961 BP NF $2.00

——The Unsinkable Mrs. Brown: S. S. Titanic Heroine. 1956 BP NF $1.25

Bancroft, Caroline, see Wills, May Bennet

Banks, John C., Colorado Law of Cities and Counties. 1961 SB NF $20.00

Bany, Amalia M., Dear Richard. Swallow Pamphlets No. 16. 1965. $1.00

Barchilon, Jacques, and Henry Pettit, The Authentic Mother Goose Fairy Tales and Nursery Rhymes. 1960 $3.75; Swallow Paperbook No. 21, $1.85

Bard, Floyd C. and Agnes Wright Spring, Dude Wrangler: Hunter: Line Rider. 1964 SB NF $3.50; $1.35 Pa.

Beatty, John Louis, Warwick and Holland. 1965 Books of Renaissance Series. NF $6.50

Beck, Warren, The Rest Is Silence. Swallow Paperbooks No. 46. 1963 F $1.65

Bell, Inglis and Baird, Donald, The English Novel 1578-1956: A Checklist of Twentieth Century Criticisms. 1959 B $3.00; Swallow Paperbooks No. 43 $1.65

Bellamann, Katherine, Two Sides of a Poem. New Poetry Series No. 11. P $2.00

Bennett, E. L., and Agnes Wright Spring, Boom Town Boy. 1967 SB NF $5.00

Bennett, Edna Mae, Turquoise and the Indian. 1966 SB NF $5.00

Bentley, Nelson, Sea Lion Caves

and Other Poems. 1966 New Poetry Series No. 35 $2.00

Black, Charles, Telescopes and Islands. 1963 New Poetry Series No. 26 $2.00

Bledsoe, Thomas, Dear Uncle Bramwell. Swallow Paperbooks No. 51. 1963 F $1.65

——Meanwhile Back at the Henhouse. 1966 F $3.95

Bobrowski, Johannes, Shadow Land. 1966 Poetry Europe Series. $2.50

Bollinger, Edward T. and Frederick Bauer, The Moffat Road. 1962 SB NF signed, numbered edition $10.00 (?)

Bonney, Orrin H. and Lorraine Bonney, Field Book: The Absaroka Range; Yellowstone Park. $2.00

——Field Book: The Teton Range. 1963 SB NF $3.50

——Field Book: Wind River Range. 1962 SB NF $3.50

——Guide to the Wyoming Mountains and Wilderness Areas. 1965 rev. ed. SB NF $7.50

Bowers, Edgar, The Form of Loss. New Poetry Series No. 13. P $2.00

——The Astronomers, 1965 P $2.50

Boyd, Maurice, ed., William Knox: His Legacy to Lincoln. 1966 SB P $5.00

Brashers, H. C., The Other Side of Love. Swallow Paperbooks No. 49. 1963 F $1.65

Breck, Allen D., The Episcopal Church in Colorado, 1860-1962. 1963 NF $10.00

Breck, Allen duPont, William Gray Evans, 1855-1924. 1964 NF BMP West in Amer. Hist. series 4. $5.00

Breihan, Carl W., Quantrill and His Civil War Guerrillas. 1959 SB NF $3.50

Brownell, Sam, Rodeos and "Tipperary." 1963 NF $2.50

Burke, J. F., Noah. 1967 F $5.75

Butcher, S. D., Pioneer History of Custer County. 1965 SB NF $8.50

Campbell, Rosemae Wells, Crystal River Valley: Jewel or Jinx? 1966 SB NF Colorado Booklets No. 7. $1.50

Cardona-Hine, Alvaro, The Flesh of Utopia. 1966 P $3.00

——The Gathering Wave. 1961 P Swallow Paperbook No. 23, .75

Carhart, Arthur H., Fishing in the West. 1960 SB NF $3.00

Carrier, Constance, The Middle Voice. Lamont Poetry Selection for 1954. P $2.00

Carroll, Donald, ed., New Poets of Ireland. 1963 P $3.50; Swallow Paperbooks No. 44 $1.65

Cassin, Maxine, A Touch of Recognition. 1962 New Poetry Series No. 25. $2.00

Centennial Symposium: The Responsible Individual in a Free Society in an Expanding Universe. 1965 BMP NF $7.50; paper edition $3.75

Chandler, Allison, Trolley through the Countryside. 1963 SB NF $12.50

Chrisman, Harry E., The Ladder of Rivers: The Story of I. P. (Print) Olive. Rev. ed. 1965 SB NF $6.00

——Lost Trails of the Cimarron. Rev. ed. 1964. SB NF $5.00

Clairmonte, Glenn, Calamity Was the Name for Jane. 1959 SB NF $3.75; WSP $1.85

Coble, John, Two Eagles. Swallow Paperbooks No. 48. 1963 F $1.65

Colegrove, Harriet, Index to Little Magazines, annual indexes for years 1948, 1949, 1950, 1951, 1952, all five reprinted 1964. Each $2.50

Coleman, Arthur, and Gary R. Taylor, Drama Criticism: A Checklist of Interpretation Since 1940 of English and American Plays. 1966 $7.50

Collier, John, From Every Zenith. 1963 NF $6.50

——On the Gleaming Way. 1962 SB NF $3.50; WSP $1.85

Collins, Dabney Otis, Great Western Rides. 1961 SB NF $4.75

Cornelius, Temple H., Sheepherder's Gold. 1964 SB NF $4.50

Crampton, Frank A., Legend of John Lamoigne. .50

Cunningham, J. V., The Exclusions of a Rhyme: Poems and Epigrams. 1960 Swallow Paperbooks No. 9, $1.35; clothbound $3.00

——Tradition and Poetic Structure. 1960 NF $4.00

——The Journal of John Cardan. 1964 NF & P $2.50

——The Judge Is Fury, 1947 P $2.00

——To What Strangers, What Welcome. 1964 P $1.75

——Woe or Wonder: The Emotional Effect of Shakespearean Tragedy. 1965 NF Swallow Paperbook No. 67 $1.35

Dallas, Sandra, Gaslights and Gingerbread. 1965 SB NF $5.00

Daney, Isabel Anderson, Pueblo's First Cross. 1966 BMP $4.50

Daniels, Bettie Marie and Virginia McConnell, The Springs of Manitou. Colo. Booklets 3. 1964 $1.65

Daryush, Elizabeth, Selected Poems. P $2.50

Davis, Sally and Betty Baldwin, Denver Dwellings and Descendants. 1963 SB NF $5.00

Desai, Ram, ed., Christianity in Africa as Seen by the Africans. 1962 NF $3.50; Swallow Paperbooks No. 40, $1.65

Dewey, John, The Public and Its Problems. NF Swallow Paperbook No. 11, $1.45; clothbound, $2.50

Dodge, Grenville M., The Battle of Atlanta. 1965 SB NF $5.00; Western Sage Paperbooks $1.75

——How We Built the Union Pacific Railway. 1964 SB NF $5.00; paper $2.50

——Personal Recollections of Lincoln, Grant, Sherman. 1965 SB NF $6.00; $1.85 paper

Draper, Wanetta W. see Hunt, Inez

Drummond, Donald F., The Battlement. P $2.50

——The Drawbridge. 1962 P $2.50

——The Grey Tower, 1966 P $3.00

duPont, Marcella, Definitions and Criteria. 1965 P $2.50

Durrell, L.W. See Harrington, H.D.

Eberhart, Perry, and Philip Schmuck. The Fourteeners. 1967 SB NF Colorado Booklets No. 8 $1.65

Eberhart, Perry, Guide to the Colorado Ghost Towns and Mining Camps. 3rd ed. 1964. SB NF $6.50

——Treasure Tales of the Rockies. Rev. ed. 1964. SB NF $5.00

Edwards, Ross, Fiddle Dust. 1965 BMP $2.95

Experiment Theatre I. EP drama $2.50

Feikema, Feike. See Manfred, Frederick

Fields, Kenneth, see Winters, Yvor

Fisher, Vardis, Adam and the Serpent. Testament of Man Series No. 4. F $3.50

——A Goat for Azazel: A novel of Christian Origins. Testament of Man Series 9. F $3.95

——April. F $3.50

——Darkness and the Deep. Testament of Man Series No. 1. F $3.50

——The Divine Passion. Testament of Man Series No. 5. F $3.50

——God or Caesar? The Writing of Fiction for Beginners. NF $5.00

——The Golden Rooms. Testament of Man Series No. 2. F $3.50

——Intimations of Eve. Testament of Man Series No. 3. F $3.50

——The Island of the Innocent. Testament of Man Series No. 7. F Swallow Paperbook No. 14, $1.95; clothbound, $3.50

——Jesus Came Again: A Parable. Testament of Man Series No. 8. F Swallow Paperbook No. 15. $1.95; clothbound, $3.95

——The Mothers. F $2.75; WSP $1.00

——My Holy Satan. Testament of Man Series No. 11. $3.95

——Orphans in Gethsemane. Testament of Man Series No. 12. 1960 F $10.00

——Peace Like a River: A Novel of Christian Asceticism. Test. of Man Series No. 10. F $3.95

——Suicide or Murder? The Strange Death of Governor Meriwether Lewis. 1962 SB NF $4.95

——Thomas Wolfe As I Knew Him and Other Essays. 1963 NF $4.00

——Valley of Vision. Testament of Man Series No. 6. F Swallow Paperbook No. 13, $1.95; clothbound, $3.95

Fitzell, Lincoln, Selected Poems. P $2.75

Fletcher, Ernest M., The Way-

——The Moral Measure of Literature. 1960 NF $3.00

McShane, Edward J., John L. Kelley, and Franklin V. Reno, Exterior Ballistics. NF $12.00

Meiners, R. K., The Last Alternatives: A Study of the Works of Allen Tate. 1963 NF $4.50

Mellard, Rudolph, Across the Crevasse. 1965 SB F $4.75

——South by Southwest. 1960 SB F $3.50

Meyers, Joan Simpson, Poetry and a Libretto. New Poetry Series No. 29. 1965 P $2.00

Miller, Nina Hull, Shutters West. 1962 SB NF $3.50

Mintz, Ruth Finer, The Darkening Green. 1965 BMP P $3.75

Mo'oney, Michael F., Francois Mauriac: A Critical Study. NF $3.75

Moyer, Claire B., Kee-Wee-Naw. 1966 BMP $7.50

Moore, Austin L., My Career as a Knight Errant. 1965 BMP NF $2.50

Morris, Clarence, How Lawyers Think. 1962 Swallow Paperbooks No. 33 NF $1.45

Morse, Samuel French, The Changes. 1964 P $3.75

Mumey, Nolie, Professor Goldrick and His Denver. 1959 SB NF .50

Murphy, E. J., The Movement West. SB NF $4.50

Naeve, Lowell, Phantasies of a Prisoner. F and art. $5.00

Naeve, Virginia, ed., Changeover: The Drive for Peace. $3.75; Swallow Paperbook No. 38. 1963 NF $1.85

——Friends of the Hibakusha. 1964 NF $4.75; Swallow Paperbook No. 66 $2.00

Nardi, Marcia, Poems. New Poetry Series No. 16 P $2.00

Nemiro, Beverly Anderson and Donna Miller Hamilton, Colorado a la Carte: second series. 1966 SB NF $3.50; paper $1.85

Nemiro, Beverly Anderson and Allmen, Marie Von, Lunchbox Cookbook. 1965 SB NF $2.95

Nin, Anais, A Spy in the House of Love. 1966 F $3.50; Swallow Paperbooks No. 82, $1.45

——Children of the Albatross. 1966 F $3.50; Swallow Paperbooks No. 80, $1.45

——Collages. 1964 F $3.75; Swallow Paperbook No. 62 $1.65

——D. H. Lawrence: An Unprofessional Study. 1964 NF $3.75; Swallow Paperbook No. 58 $1.65

——The Four-Chambered Heart. 1966 F $3.50; Swallow Paperbooks No. 81, $1.45

——House of Incest. 1961 F Swallow Paperbook No. 31, $1.00

——Ladders to Fire. 1966 F $3.50; Swallow Paperbooks No. 79, $1.45

——Seduction of the Minotaur. 1961 F Swallow Paperbook No. 28, $1.65; cloth $3.75

——Under a Glass Bell. 1961 F Swallow Paperbook No. 30, $1.00

——Winter of Artifice. 1961 F Swallow Paperbook No. 29, $1.45; cloth $3.50

Nixon, Lucille M. and Tomoe Tana, eds., Sounds from the Unknown. 1964 P $3.75; Swallow Paperbook No. 60 $1.75

Norse, Harold, The Undersea Mountain. New Poetry Series No. 8. P $2.00

O'Hagan, The Woman Who Got On at Jasper Station. Swallow Paperbooks No. 53. 1963 F $1.65

One Hundred Years of Alaska Poetry. 1966 P $3.75

Ormes, Robert M., Guide to the Colorado Mountains. 1966 ed. SB NF $3.50

——Railroads and the Rockies. 1963 SB NF $6.50

Osborn, Mary Elizabeth, Who Tempers the Wind. Swallow Paperbooks No. 47. 1963 F $1.65

Packard, William, In the First Place. 1960 EP $1.50

——On the Other Hand. 1963 EP $1.50

——Once & For All. 1962 EP play $1.50

——To Peel an Apple. 1964 EP P $1.50

Parkhill, Forbes, The Law Goes West. SB NF $2.50

——Mister Barney Ford. 1963 SB NF $4.50; Western Sage Paperbooks, $1.85

Parkhill, Forbes. See also Fletcher, Ernest M.

Parliamentary Procedure. NF .50; quantity prices

Pauker, John, Yoked by Violence. New Poetry Series No. 2. P $2.00

Payne, Stephen, Where the Rockies Ride Herd. 1965 SB NF $5.75

Peake, Ora Brooks, A History of the United States Indian Factory System. SB NF $5.00

Pearl, Richard M., America's Mountain: Pikes Peak and the Pikes Peak Region. 1964 SB NF Colorado Booklets No. 4 $1.00

——Colorado Gem Trails and Mineral Guide. Rev. ed. 1965 SB NF $3.95

——Colorado Rocks, Minerals, Fossils. 1964 SB NF $3.95

Pendleton, Conrad, West: Manhattan to Oregon. P 1966 $3.50

Perry, Ronald, The Rock Harbor. 1960 New Poetry Series No. 21. P $2.00

Petrarca, Adela R., Withhold Not the West. 1966 SB NF $5.75

Pettit, Henry—see Barchilon, J.

Pickard, Cynthia, Woman in Apartment. New Poetry Series No. 17. P $2.00

Pillin, William, Pavanne for a Fading Memory. 1964 P $3.00

Planz, Allen, Pan American. 1966 New Poetry Series No. 36. $2.50

Porter, R. Russell, The University of Denver Centennial: Its Philosophy, Preparation, Presentation. 1965 BMP NF $2.50

Raitt, Helen, Exploring the Deep Pacific. 1964 SB NF $4.00; WSP $1.95

Ramsey, Gerald, Morning, Noon and Night Cookbook. 1963 SB NF $4.75

Read, Effie O., White Pine Lang Syne. 1965 BMP NF $6.50

Readings on Fascism and National Socialism. NF Swallow Paperbook No. 3, $1.35

Reeve, Frank, New Mexico: A Short History. Southwest Series No. 3. 1964 $2.00; cloth, $3.00

Renken, Maxine, A Bibliography of Henry Miller: 1945-1961. 1962

Swallow Pamphlets No. 12. B .50

Reno, Franklin V. See McShane, Edward J.

Reno, Philip, And Farther On Was Gold. 1962 Southwest Series No. 1. $1.00

——Taos Pueblo. 1963 Southwest Series No. 2. $1.00

Riddell, Joseph N., Jackson R. Bryan, and Samuel French Morse, Wallace Stevens Checklist and Bibliography of Stevens Criticism. 1963 B $3.50

Robertson, Frank C.—See Harris, Beth Kay

Robins, Natalie S., My Father Spoke of His Riches. 1966 P Swallow Paperbooks No. 72. $.75

——Wild Lace. 1960 P Swallow Paperbook No. 19, .75

Rockwell, Wilson, Memoirs of a Lawman. 1962 SB NF $5.00

——Uncompahgre Country. 1965 SB NF $6.50

Rosenberg, James L., A Primer of Kinetics. 1962 New Poetry Series No. 24. P $2.00

Roth, Charles B., C. T.—Sage of the Rockies. 1960 SB NF Limited, signed edition, $2.00

Rouse, J. E., The World's Cattle, Vol. 1. 1967 BMP $10.00

Russell, Mrs. Hal, Settler Mac and the Charmed Quarter-Section. NF $2.50

Russell, William, Jr.—See Hollenback, F. R.

Sankey, Benjamin, The Major Novels of Thomas Hardy. 1965 NF $2.50

Schevill, James, The Black President and Other Plays. 1965 $5.75; Swallow Paperbooks No. 74. $2.50

——Private Dooms and Public Destinations: Poems 1945-1962. 1962 Swallow Paperbooks No. 36. P $1.65

——The Stalingrad Elegies. 1964 P $2.75; Swallow Paperbook No. 59 $1.65

Seligson, Harry and George Bardwell, Labor-Management Relations in Colorado. 1961 SB NF $6.00

Senior, Willoughby F., Smoke Upon

NF $3.00; Wyoming Booklets No. 4 $2.00

Urbanek, Mae and Urbanek, Jerry, The Uncovered Wagon. SB NF $3.50

Vaux, Thomas Lord—see Vonalt, L. P.

Voltaire, The Virgin of Orleans, trans. Howard Nelson. 1965. Forgotten Classics series. NF $5.00

Vonalt, Larry P., ed., Poems of Lord Vaux. 1960 Books of the Renaissance Series, P $2.00

Wallace, Betty, Gunnison. 1964 SB NF Colorado Booklets No. 5 $1.50

——History with the Hide Off. 1965 SB NF $4.50

Wallis, George A., Cattle Kings of the Staked Plains. 1965 SB NF $4.00

Wantling, William, From the Jungle's Edge. 1966 P Swallow Paperbooks No. 84, $.75

Warren, James E., Jr., The Teacher of English, His Materials and Opportunities. NF Swallow Paperbook No. 4, $1.35

Waters, Frank, Man Who Killed the Deer. SB F $3.00; WSP $1.85 (American Library Series)

——Masked Gods. 1962 SB NF $5.75

——People of the Valley. 1962 SB F $3.50; WSP $1.85

——Pumpkin Seed Point. 1967 NF $4.50

——The Woman at Otowi Crossing. 1966 F $4.95

Wearin, Otha D., Statues That Pour. 1965 SB NF $6.00

Weber, Lenora Mattingly, see Hi b, Greta

Wilcox, Virginia Lee, Colorado: A Selected Bibliography from 1858 through 1952. SB B $5.00

Williams, John, The Broken Landscape. New Poetry Series No. 3, P $2.00

Wills, May Bennett, and Caroline Bancroft, The Unsinkable Molly Brown Cookbook. 1966 NF $2.00

Winters, Yvor, The Brink of Darkness. 1965. F Swallow Pamphlets No. 16. $.50

——Collected Poems. P Swallow Paperbook No. 10, $1.65; clothbound $3.50

——The Early Poems of Yvor Winters. 1966 P $3.50

——Forms of Discovery: Critical and Historical Essays on the Forms of the Short Poem in English. 1967 NF $7.50

——The Function of Criticism: Problems and Exercises. NF $3.00; Swallow Paperbook No. 83. $1.85

——In Defense of Reason. Contemporary Critics Series. NF $6.00; Swallow Paperbook No. 69. $3.75

——The Poetry of J. V. Cunningham. 1961 Swallow Pamphlets No. 11. NF .50

——The Poetry of W. B. Yeats. 1960 Swallow Pamphlets No. 10. NF .50

Winters, Yvor, and Kenneth Fields, eds., The Quest for Reality: A Critical Anthology of the Short Poem in English. 1967 P $6.00

Wolle, Muriel Sibell, Montana Pay Dirt. 1963 NF SB $12.50

——Stampede to Timberline. 1962 NF SB $7.50

Woodford, Bruce P., Twenty-One Poems and a Play. P $2.50

Wright, Arthur, The Civil War in the Southwest. 1964. BMP NF $5.00

Wright, Celeste T., Etruscan Princess and Other Poems. New Poetry Series No. 27. 1964 P $2.00

Wright, E izabeth V. See Thurston, Jarvis

Yarber, Esther, Land of the Yankee Fork. 1963 NF SB $4.00

Young, A. Beatrice, The Epiphany Story. 1965 BMP $3.50

Yost, Nellie Snyder, The Call of the Range: Story of the Nebraska Stock Growers Association. 1966 SB NF $10.00

Zamonski, Stanley W., and Teddy Keller, The Fifty-Niners: A Denver Diary. 1961 SB NF $4.50 WSP $1.85